EASY PIES
TARTS &
QUICHES

Publisher: Ray Ramsay
Editors: Margaret Gore and Joy Hayes
UK Cookery Editor: Katie Swallow
Sub-editor: Ann Smith
Production Manager: Anna Maguire
Design: John Bull and Karen Jeffery
Cover Design: Chrissie Lloyd
Home Economists: Susan Brazel and Susan Bell
Cover Home Economist: Kay McGlone
Food Stylists: Susan Brazel and Judith Minahan
Cover Stylist: Kathy Man
Photography: Phil Wymant
Cover Photography: Gus Filgate

Typeset at The Typographers, North Sydney, NSW

Printed at Griffin Press Limited, Netley, South Australia

ISBN 1-875216-33-2

**Published by The Custom Book Company
15B Penrhyn Avenue, Beecroft, NSW 2119

© Custom Book Company

Distributed by J.B. Fairfax Press Ltd
9 Trinity Centre, Park Farm Estate
Wellingborough, Northants, UK
Ph: (0933) 402330 Fax: (0933) 402234

**A joint venture of Century Magazines Pty Limited
and R.A. Ramsay Pty Limited

EASY PIES, TARTS & QUICHES

Welcome to *Easy Pies, Tarts & Quiches*, a cookbook that makes it easy as pie to fit great cookery into a busy lifestyle. Now you can show off your culinary skills with stylish, savoury and sweet baked pastry treats. You can't go wrong with these wonderful recipes using puff, filo and shortcrust pastries from your freezer.

All the recipes in this book are quick to prepare, using readily available ingredients, and range from exotic dinner party fare to economical family meals and tempting snacks.

Happy cooking – you'll rise to any occasion with these exciting recipes!

CONTENTS

Oriental Chicken Rolls   Recipe, page 8

QUICK FINGER FOODS

Here comes a feast of savouries in appetising shapes, sizes
and flavours. These delectable little pastry-based finger snacks
are quick and easy to prepare – fast favourites for parties, picnics
and family gatherings, with hot or cold drinks. Freeze them
ahead or serve them straight from the oven and watch
them disappear. That's easy!

Pizza Savouries

Pizza Savouries

2 tablespoons olive oil
3 tablespoons finely chopped fresh basil
2 tablespoons chopped fresh chives
1 teaspoon dried oregano
1 clove garlic, crushed
1 ready-made pizza base
olives
cherry tomatoes, halved
rolled anchovies

1. Combine oil, herbs and garlic; mix well.
2. Place pizza base on a pizza tray or baking sheet. Spread herb mixture evenly over pizza base.
3. Bake in a very hot oven for 10–15 minutes or until base is crisp.
4. Cut into squares or shapes, and garnish with olives, tomatoes and anchovies. Serve hot.

Total preparation and cooking time: 25 minutes

This recipe does not freeze.

Oriental Chicken Rolls

Don't forget the dipping sauce!

750g/1½lb lean chicken mince
6 shallots or spring onions, chopped
1 small green capsicum (pepper), chopped
1 cup/60g/2oz. fresh breadcrumbs
1 clove garlic, crushed
1 teaspoon finely chopped fresh ginger
pepper, to taste
2 teaspoons dry sherry, optional
2 tablespoons soy sauce
500g/1lb puff pastry, thawed
beaten egg for glazing

MAKES APPROXIMATELY 16 (depending on size)

1. Combine chicken, shallots, capsicum, breadcrumbs, garlic, ginger, pepper, sherry and soy sauce. Mix well.
2. Cut pastry into 2 and roll out each piece to an oblong 38cm x 15cm/15in. x 6in. Lightly brush pastry with water.
3. Using a teaspoon, spoon a portion of filling down the middle of the pastry strip. Fold pastry over filling and seal edges.
4. With a sharp knife, cut each strip into 8 rolls.
5. Continue with remaining filling and pastry. Glaze.
6. Place on an ungreased baking tray. Bake in a very hot oven for 20 minutes or until golden.

Dipping sauce

2 teaspoons cornflour
1 tablespoon brown sugar
1 teaspoon finely chopped fresh ginger
1 tablespoon soy sauce
¼ cup/60ml/2fl. oz. tomato sauce
¼ cup/60ml/2fl. oz. water

1. Place cornflour and sugar in a small saucepan. Combine ginger, soy sauce, tomato sauce and water, then gradually blend into the cornflour mixture.
2. Stir constantly over gentle heat until mixture thickens and boils. Serve hot or cold.
To microwave:
Blend all ingredients together in a microwave-safe jug. Cook on high (100% power) for 2 minutes. Stir occasionally.

Total preparation and cooking time: 50 minutes

The chicken rolls will freeze well, but not the sauce.

Pizza Pinwheels

Pizza Pinwheels

Mamma mia, they're good!

250g/8oz. puff pastry, thawed
⅓ cup/75ml/2½fl. oz. tomato paste (purée)
1 tablespoon freshly chopped mixed herbs
4 rashers bacon, finely chopped
2 tablespoons olives, finely chopped
¼ cup/30g/1oz. grated parmesan cheese
beaten egg for glazing

MAKES APPROXIMATELY 25 PINWHEELS

1. Roll out pastry to an oblong 33cm x 20cm/ 13in. x 8in. Spread pastry with tomato paste and sprinkle with herbs, bacon, olives and cheese.
2. Roll up pastry, starting at the long edge. Using a sharp knife, cut into 1cm/½in. slices and place on a lightly greased baking sheet. Glaze.

3. Bake in a very hot oven for 12–15 minutes or until pastry is golden.

Total preparation and cooking time: 25 minutes

Variation: *Crab Pinwheels*

⅓ cup/80g/2½oz. prepared seafood dip
170g/5½oz. can crabmeat, well drained
2 shallots or spring onions, finely chopped
½ teaspoon dried thyme
seasoning to taste

1. Spread dip on unrolled pastry, sprinkle with remaining ingredients and proceed as above.

These pinwheels freeze well. Cook from frozen on the day they are required.

Fish Cocktails

Fish Cocktails

Delicious fun

1 small onion, finely chopped
1 tablespoon capers, optional
⅓ cup/80g/2½oz. tomato paste (purée)
¼ teaspoon dried dill
1 teaspoon lemon pepper
2 sheets puff pastry, thawed
200g/6½oz. white fish fillets, sliced into
2cm x 3cm/¾in. x 1¼in. strips
beaten egg for glazing

MAKES 12 FISH

1. Combine onion, capers, tomato paste, dill and lemon pepper. Mix well.
2. Roll out each sheet of pastry thinly. Cut a fish shape, 9cm x 4cm/3½in. x 2in. out of heavy cardboard. Using this as a template, cut 12 fish out of each sheet of pastry.
3. Place a teaspoonful of tomato mixture on half the fish shapes; top with a strip of fish. Place remaining pastry fish shapes on top; decorate the fish shapes with a sharp knife, if desired. Glaze.
4. Bake in a very hot oven for 5–8 minutes or until puffed and golden.

Total preparation and cooking time: 40 minutes

This recipe does not freeze.

Sausage Rolls

3 slices bread, crusts removed
½ cup/125ml/4fl. oz. hot water
1kg/2lb sausage meat
1 onion, finely chopped
½ teaspoon dried mixed herbs
salt and pepper to taste
500g/1lb puff pastry, thawed
beaten egg for glazing

MAKES APPROXIMATELY 12 (depending on size)

1. Remove crusts from bread, then soak slices in hot water for 5 minutes. Squeeze out excess water.
2. Combine bread, sausage meat, onion, herbs and seasonings. Mix well.
3. Roll out pastry thinly to a large oblong, then cut lengthwise into 2 strips.
4. Using a teaspoon, spoon a portion of meat mixture down the middle of each pastry strip. Brush edges of pastry with water, then fold pastry over filling and seal edges.
5. With a sharp knife cut each strip into 6 sausage rolls. Glaze.
6. Place on an ungreased baking tray. Bake in a very hot oven for 15–20 minutes or until golden.

Total preparation and cooking time: 45 minutes

This recipe freezes very well unbaked. Cook from frozen, increasing baking time by 5 minutes.

Tuna & Spinach Rolls

250g/8oz. packet frozen spinach, thawed
and drained
410g/13oz. can tuna, drained
1 small onion, finely chopped
2 tablespoons mayonnaise
black pepper to taste
315g/10oz. shortcrust pastry, thawed
beaten egg for glazing

MAKES 16

1. Combine spinach, tuna, onion, mayonnaise and pepper; mix well. Cut pastry in half and roll out each piece to an oblong 38cm x 15cm/15in. x 6in. Spoon tuna mixture down the middle of each pastry strip.
2. Brush edges of pastry with water and roll pastry over the filling. Seal edge firmly.
3. Using a sharp knife, cut each pastry roll into 8. Place rolls on a lightly greased baking tray. Glaze.
4. Bake in a moderate oven for 30–35 minutes or until golden brown.

Total preparation and cooking time: 45 minutes

This recipe does not freeze.

Sausage Rolls
Tuna and Spinach Rolls

Camembert & Asparagus Puffs
Cheese Pretzels
Spinach & Cheese Triangles
Recipe, page 14

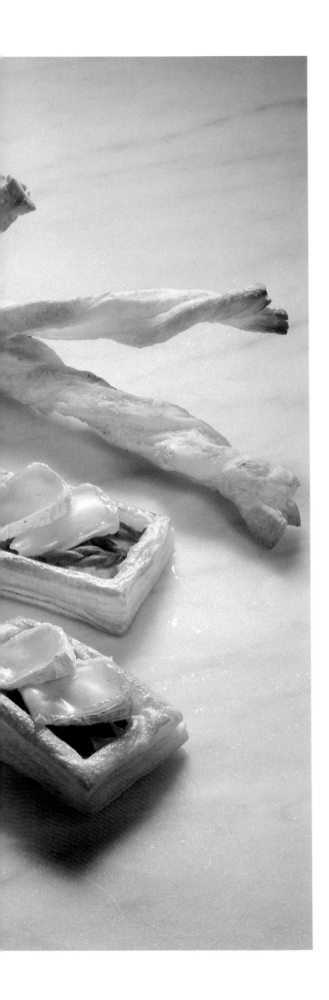

Camembert & Asparagus Puffs

2 sheets puff pastry, thawed
15 spears fresh asparagus, blanched and cooled
2 x 125g/4oz. camembert cheeses, cut into wedges
beaten egg for glazing
fresh chives for garnish

MAKES 15

1. Roll out each sheet of pastry thinly and cut into 15 strips (10cm x 6cm/4in. x 2½in.).
2. Cut centres from half the pastry strips, leaving a 1cm/½in. border.
3. Brush the full strips of pastry with water; place the remaining strips on top.
4. Cut asparagus spears to fit the centre of the pastry; top with sliced cheese. Glaze edges.
5. Bake in a very hot oven for 10 minutes or until pastry is golden. Serve immediately.

Total preparation and cooking time: 35 minutes

This recipe does not freeze.

PASTRY TIP

When cutting pastry with a knife or cutters, cut with one clean motion. Do not drag the knife or twist the cutter, otherwise the layers and 'lift' of the pastry will be affected.

Cheese Pretzels

6 sheets puff pastry, thawed
15g/½oz. butter or margarine, melted
1 cup/125g/4oz. finely grated cheese
¼ cup/30g/1oz. finely grated parmesan cheese

MAKES 20

1. Roll out sheets of pastry thinly, then brush 3 sheets with melted butter or margarine.
2. Combine cheeses; sprinkle over buttered pastry.
3. Top with remaining pastry sheets, pressing down gently. Brush top surface with butter or margarine.
4. With a sharp knife, cut pastry into 20 strips. Form pretzels by twisting several times. Place on an ungreased baking tray.
5. Bake in a very hot oven for 10–15 minutes or until golden brown.

Total preparation and cooking time: 25 minutes

This recipe freezes well.

Spinach & Cheese Triangles

With love from Greece

250g/8oz. frozen spinach, thawed and well drained
125g/4oz. ricotta cheese
125g/4oz. fetta cheese, crumbled
1 shallot or spring onion, finely chopped
pinch nutmeg
9 sheets filo pastry, thawed
1 tablespoon polyunsaturated oil

MAKES 18

1. Combine spinach, ricotta, fetta, shallots or spring onions, and nutmeg. Mix well.
2. Cut filo pastry sheets into 6 strips using 3 strips for each triangle. Brush every second layer lightly with oil.
3. Place a teaspoonful of mixture near the bottom right-hand corner of each strip and fold the corner over to form a triangle. Continue folding to end of strip, retaining triangle shape with each fold.
4. Place seam side down on an ungreased baking sheet. Brush tops lightly with oil.
5. Bake in a moderately hot oven for 15–20 minutes or until pastry is golden.

Total preparation and cooking time: 45 minutes

Alternative filling: *Cheese and Nut Triangle*

125g/4oz. ricotta cheese
125g/4oz. fetta cheese
¼ cup/30g/1oz. pine nuts
1 shallot or spring onion, finely chopped
1 teaspoon minced chilli
1 egg, beaten

1. Combine all ingredients and proceed as above.

This recipe is suitable to freeze. Prepare up to the baking stage; freeze unbaked. On day of serving, cook from frozen, increasing baking time by 5 minutes.

Mini Quiches

2 sheets puff pastry, thawed
1 onion, finely chopped
1–2 rashers bacon, finely chopped
½ cup/60g/2oz. grated cheese
2 eggs
½ cup/125ml/4fl. oz. milk
seasoning to taste

Mini Quiches

MAKES 24

1. Roll out each sheet of pastry thinly. Using a 6.5cm/2¾in. scone cutter, cut 24 rounds of pastry and use to line 24 dome-shaped patty tins.
2. Divide onion, bacon and cheese between the patty tins. Combine eggs, milk and seasoning. Beat well with a fork.
3. Pour the egg mixture carefully into the pastry cases.
4. Bake in a hot oven 15–20 minutes or until golden and puffed. Serve warm.

Total preparation and cooking time: 50 minutes

Variation: *Mushroom Quiches*

1 cup/60g/2oz. finely chopped mushrooms
15g/½oz. butter or margarine
½ cup/60g/2oz. grated cheese
½ cup/125ml/4fl. oz. cream
2 eggs
seasoning to taste

1. Lightly sauté mushrooms and butter (or microwave 1 minute on high (100% power); cool.
2. Divide mushrooms and cheese between the patty tins. Combine cream, eggs and seasoning. Proceed as above.

Variation: *Oyster Quiches*

100g/3½oz. can smoked oysters, well drained and chopped
½ cup/60g/2oz. grated cheese
1 tablespoon finely chopped fresh dill
½ cup/125ml/4fl. oz. milk
2 eggs

1. Divide oysters and cheese between patty tins. Combine dill, milk and eggs. Proceed as above.

This recipe freezes well. Bake the quiches and allow to cool before freezing. Reheat in a moderate oven when required.

Blue Cheese Tarts

Great with drinks

125g/4oz. puff pastry, thawed
75g/2½oz. creamy blue cheese
2 tablespoons cream
1 egg
1 teaspoon chopped fresh chives
ground black pepper

MAKES APPROXIMATELY 18

1. Roll out pastry and cut into rounds using a 6–7.5cm/2½–3in. cutter. Place pastry rounds in dome-shaped patty tins.
2. In a blender or food processor combine cheese, cream, egg, chives and pepper. Mix well.
3. Spoon one tablespoon of mixture into each pastry case.
4. Bake in a hot oven for 12–15 minutes or until puffed and golden. Serve warm.

Total preparation and cooking time: 30 minutes

This recipe does not freeze.

Mini Spring Rolls

From your kitchen takeaway

1 tablespoon oil
6 shallots or spring onions, finely chopped
2 teaspoons fresh ginger, finely chopped
185g/6oz. pork or veal mince
185g/6oz. raw, peeled prawns, chopped
1 cup/125g/4oz. finely chopped celery
¼ small Chinese or savoy cabbage, shredded
1½ cups/90g/3oz. sliced mushrooms
½ cup/60g/2oz. sliced capsicum (pepper)
2 tablespoons sherry, optional
2 tablespoons soy sauce
280g/10oz. filo pastry, thawed
¼ cup/60ml/2fl. oz. polyunsaturated oil

MAKES APPROXIMATELY 16

1. Heat oil, add shallots or spring onions and ginger, and cook for 1 minute. Stir in the pork or veal mince; cook, stirring continuously, until evenly browned. Add prawns, celery, cabbage, mushrooms, capsicum, sherry and soy sauce; cook over gentle heat until water has evaporated. Cool.
2. Cut pastry sheets into quarters. Using 3 of the quarters of pastry for each roll, brush each lightly with oil and layer.
3. Place 1 tablespoon of mixture on bottom edge of pastry; roll up. Continue with remaining pastry and filling. Brush rolls lightly with oil.

Mini Spring Rolls

4. Place on a lightly greased baking sheet. Bake in a moderate oven 10–15 minutes or until golden and crisp. Serve with Plum Dipping Sauce.

Total preparation and cooking time: 45 minutes

This recipe is suitable to freeze. Prepare up to the baking stage; freeze unbaked. On day of serving, cook from frozen, increasing baking time by 5 minutes.

Plum Dipping Sauce

1 tablespoon oil
1 onion, finely chopped
2 teaspoons finely chopped fresh ginger
1 teaspoon minced chilli
1 tablespoon soy sauce
1 cup/250g/8oz. plum conserve
1 tablespoon white vinegar
1 tablespoon cornflour
¼ cup/60ml/2fl. oz. water

1. Heat oil, add onion, ginger and chilli, and cook for 2–3 minutes. Add soy sauce, plum conserve and vinegar. Blend cornflour and water together and stir into sauce. Continue cooking and stirring until mixture boils and thickens. Cook 1 minute.

Vol-au-Vents

500g/1lb puff pastry, thawed
beaten egg for glazing

MAKES APPROXIMATELY 30 (bite-sized)

1. Cut pastry into 3 equal pieces. Roll out each piece of pastry to 2.5mm/⅛in. thickness.
2. Using a 5cm/2in. round, oval or square cutter, and even pressure, cut 30 discs from one piece of pastry. Turn discs upside-down on an ungreased baking sheet.
3. Lightly brush the second piece of pastry with water and lay third piece on top.
4. Cut another 30 discs (matching the base pastry) from the two joined sheets of pastry.
5. Using a small cutter, cut an inner circle from the double layer of pastry. Carefully remove the centres and set aside.
6. Carefully place the pastry rings on the bases.
7. With a fork, prick the base pastry.
8. Brush the top surface of rings lightly with egg glaze.
9. Bake in a very hot oven for 10 minutes or until golden.

Total preparation and cooking time: 45 minutes

Reheating instructions

The sooner the vol-au-vent cases can be filled and served, the fresher, lighter and more delicious they will be. However, they can be reheated if serving the same day, or frozen. Wrap in freezer bag or freezer wrap. Make airtight, seal, label and freeze.

To reheat unfilled

Place unfilled vol-au-vents in hot oven for 3–5 minutes. Turn off heat and within 8–10 minutes vol-au-vents will be crisp.

To reheat filled

Place filled vol-au-vents in moderate oven for 15–20 minutes.

Vol-au-Vent Fillings

Chicken and Corn

1 cup/125g/4oz. cooked, diced chicken
1 cup/125g/4oz. corn kernels
½ cup/60g/2oz. corn relish
2 tablespoons cream
½ cup/125ml/4fl. oz. prepared cheese sauce

SUFFICIENT FOR 30 BITE-SIZE VOL-AU-VENTS

1. Combine all ingredients in a small saucepan or in a microwave-safe bowl. Stir over gentle heat until cooked through, or microwave on high (100% power) for 3 minutes, stirring occasionally.

Crab

170g/5½oz. can crabmeat, well drained and flaked
⅔ cup/155g/5oz. mayonnaise
1 tablespoon lemon juice
1 teaspoon prepared mild mustard
1 teaspoon horseradish cream
½ cup/60g/2oz. finely chopped red capsicum (pepper)
ground black pepper to taste

1. Combine all ingredients in a bowl.

Mussel Delight

375g/12oz. jar marinated mussels, drained and chopped
½ cup/125ml/4fl. oz. sour cream
½ cup/125g/4oz. mayonnaise
4 shallots or spring onions, finely chopped
2 teaspoons grated lemon rind
ground black pepper

1. Combine all ingredients in a bowl.

Guacamole Tarts

Mexican moments

250g/8oz. shortcrust pastry, thawed
¾ cup/185g/6oz. avocado flesh
½ cup/125ml/4fl. oz. sour cream
3 tablespoons mayonnaise
1 tablespoon lemon juice
½ clove garlic, crushed
pinch cayenne pepper
fresh chives

MAKES APPROXIMATELY 24

1. Roll out pastry and cut into rounds using a 6–7.5cm/2½–3in. cutter. Place pastry rounds in patty tins. Prick base of pastry. Bake in a moderately hot oven for 10 minutes or until golden brown. Cool.
2. Place avocado, sour cream, mayonnaise, lemon juice, garlic and cayenne into a food processor or blender. Process until smooth.
3. Spoon or pipe avocado mixture into cooled pastry cases. Garnish with snipped chives.

Total preparation and cooking time: 30 minutes

This recipe does not freeze.

Vol-au-Vents

Apple Strudel Waffles

Snack-time, folks!

90g/3oz. shortcrust pastry, thawed
melted butter or margarine
4 tablespoons cooked or canned apples,
sweetened to taste
1 tablespoon sultanas
1 tablespoon ground almonds
mixed spice

MAKES 4 JAFFLES

1. Roll out pastry to 20cm x 15cm/8in. x 6in. Brush pastry lightly with melted butter or margarine; cut pastry in half. Place one half, buttered side down, in a heated waffle- or sandwich-maker.

2. Place apples, sultanas, almonds and mixed spice on pastry. Top with remaining pastry, buttered side up.

3. Close waffle- or sandwich-maker and cook until pastry is golden. Serve hot.

This recipe can easily be doubled to make extra waffles.

Total preparation and cooking time: 15 minutes

Variation: *Savoury Waffles*

For savoury waffles, use 1–2 tablespoons each of well-drained crushed pineapple, grated cheese and finely chopped ham.
N.B.: Puff pastry can also be used but waffle-maker must not be clipped closed.

This recipe does not freeze.

Apple Strudel Waffles

TIME-SAVING FAMILY MEALS

The busy home cook will welcome this treasury of time-saving, nourishing dishes designed to transform everyday family meals into pleasant surprises. Our exciting savoury and sweet recipes look wonderful and taste even better. Easy as pie!

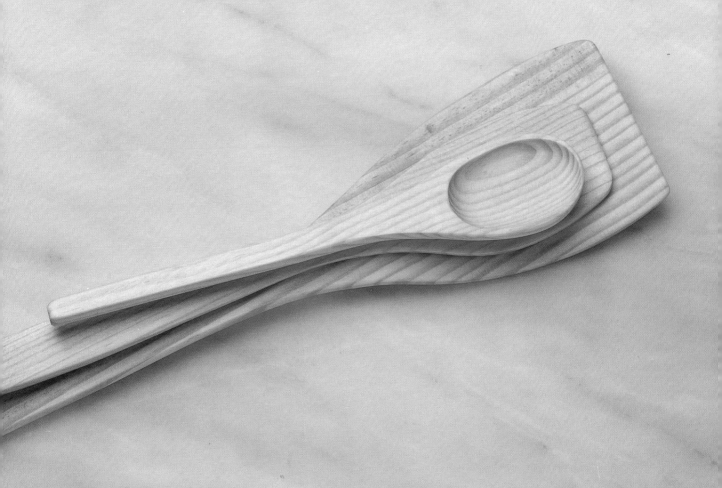

Chicken & Mushroom Pie

Chicken & Mushroom Pies

30g/1oz. butter or margarine
1 onion, finely chopped
1½ cups/90g/3oz. mushrooms, sliced
1 tablespoon plain flour
¾ cup/185ml/6fl. oz. milk
¼ cup/60ml/2fl. oz. cream
1½ cups/185g/6oz. cooked chicken, chopped
¼ teaspoon each dried rosemary and thyme
pinch nutmeg
ground black pepper
8 sheets filo pastry, thawed
2 tablespoons polyunsaturated oil
sesame seeds

SERVES 4

1. Melt half the butter, add onions and mush-rooms, and cook until tender. To microwave, place butter, onions and mushrooms in a microwave-safe bowl and cook 1 minute on high (100% power).
2. Melt remaining butter, add flour and cook 1 minute. Remove from heat and gradually stir in milk and cream. Return to heat, stirring continuously until mixture thickens and boils. Fold in mushroom mixture, chicken and seasonings. Cool.
3. Lightly brush 4 sheets of pastry with oil; layer. Cut layered pastry sheets into 4 rectangles. Place stacks of pastry into individual pie tins or ramekins, allowing pastry to overhang edges.
4. Divide chicken mixture between the 4 pies. Lightly brush remaining sheets of pastry with oil; layer. Cut into 4. Place a stack of pastry on each pie; trim edges. Sprinkle with sesame seeds.
5. Bake in a moderately hot oven for 15–20 minutes or until golden. Serve hot.

Total preparation and cooking time: 45 minutes

This recipe does not freeze.

Apricot Chicken Loaf

250g/8oz. shortcrust pastry, thawed
500g/1lb lean minced chicken
¼ cup/15g/½oz. chopped shallots or spring onions
10 canned apricot halves, chopped
2 tablespoons chopped fresh coriander or parsley
2 tablespoons mayonnaise
salt and pepper to taste
beaten egg for glazing

SERVES 4–6

1. Roll pastry out to a 30cm/12in. square. In a bowl combine chicken, shallots or spring onions, apricots, coriander or parsley, and mayonnaise. Season to taste with salt and pepper.
2. Spoon chicken mixture down centre of pastry, forming mixture into a log shape. Brush edges of pastry lightly with water. On either side of filling, make diagonal cuts at 1cm/½in. intervals, to produce 1cm/½in.-wide pastry strips. Lift alternate strips over filling, as if making a plait. Glaze with beaten egg.
3. Bake in a moderately hot oven for 40 minutes or until pastry is golden brown. Serve warm with vegetables or salad.

Total preparation and cooking time: 60 minutes

This recipe does not freeze.

PASTRY TIP

Shortcrust is a tender, crunchy, melt-in-the-mouth buttery pastry. Shortcrust gets its characteristics from the ingredient mixing. Butter or margarine is rubbed into the flour so that it is finely dispersed, without turning into a continuous paste, then lightly mixed to a soft dough with water. On baking, it is a friable, easily broken, short pastry.

Apricot Chicken Loaf

Salmon & Vegetable Pie

Salmon & Vegetable Pie

Light and easy

250g/8oz. packet frozen mixed vegetables
2 sheets puff pastry, thawed
220g/7oz. can pink salmon, well drained and flaked
2 hard-boiled eggs, sliced
½ cup/125g/4oz. mayonnaise
200g/6½oz. can whole champignons, well drained
beaten egg for glazing

SERVES 4–6

1. Cook frozen vegetables. Drain, season and allow to become cold.
2. Roll out one sheet of pastry to a 23cm/9in. square and the other to a 25cm/10in. square. Place smaller sheet of pastry on a lightly greased baking tray.
3. Spoon cold vegetables onto pastry, leaving a 3cm/1¼in. border all around. Top with salmon, eggs, mayonnaise and champignons.
4. Lightly brush pastry border with water. Top with second pastry sheet and press edges together to seal. Glaze and make a slit in centre of pie.
5. Bake in a moderately hot oven for 15–20 minutes or until pastry is golden.

Total preparation and cooking time: 35 minutes

This recipe does not freeze.

PASTRY TIP

To produce high gloss and golden colour on your pastry items, glaze with egg wash (beaten egg). Lightly beat 1 egg with 1 tablespoon cold water and ¼–½ teaspoon salt.

Minted Apricot Lamb

Minted Apricot Lamb

Sensational

625g/1¼lb lean lamb, cubed
2 tablespoons prepared mint jelly
¼ cup/30g/1oz. pecan pieces
¼ cup/30g/1oz. sliced dried apricots
½ cup/30g/1oz. chopped shallots or spring onions
1–2 sheets puff pastry, thawed
beaten egg for glazing

SERVES 4

1. In a bowl combine cubed lamb, mint jelly, pecans, apricots and shallots or spring onions. Mix well.
2. Divide mixture between 4 ovenproof ramekins.

3. Roll out pastry thinly. Place ramekins on pastry and use as a guide for cutting pastry tops 2cm/¾in. larger than ramekins.
4. Wet rims of ramekins lightly with water. Place pastry on top. Pinch edges to form a frill. Glaze with egg; cut small air-vent in top.
5. Bake in a hot oven for 20 minutes or until pastry is golden.

Total preparation and cooking time: 35 minutes

This recipe does not freeze.

PASTRY TIP

Pastry tops, as used in this recipe, are a great way to dress up soups and individual casseroles or to top stewed fruit.

Bacon & Egg Pie

Sunday night treat

250g/8oz. shortcrust pastry, thawed
3–4 rashers bacon, chopped
¼ cup/15g/½oz. chopped fresh parsley
½ cup/30g/1oz. sliced mushrooms
ground black pepper
6 eggs
beaten egg for glazing

SERVES 4–6

1. Roll out three-quarters of the pastry and use to line a 20cm/8in. pie dish. Trim edges.
2. Place bacon, parsley and mushrooms in pastry case; season with pepper. Crack eggs over filling.
3. Roll out remaining pastry and top pie with latticed or plain pastry. Trim and crimp edges. Glaze top of pie with egg. Cut a vent in the centre of pie.
4. Bake in a moderately hot oven for 25–30 minutes or until pastry is golden brown. Serve with salad or vegetables.

Total preparation and cooking time: 40 minutes

This recipe does not freeze.

Steak & Kidney Pie

750g/1½lb stewing steak, cut into cubes
2 lamb kidneys, cleaned and sliced
3 tablespoons seasoned flour
pinch nutmeg
¼ teaspoon dried thyme
1 onion, finely chopped
1 cup/250ml/8fl. oz. beef stock
(or ½ beef stock and ½ red wine)
1 bay leaf
1 tablespoon Worcestershire sauce
250g/8oz. puff pastry, thawed
beaten egg for glazing

SERVES 4–6

1. Toss meat and kidneys in seasoned flour. Place prepared meat in a pie dish; sprinkle with nutmeg, thyme, onion. Pour over beef stock; add bay leaf and Worcestershire sauce. Cover. Cook in a moderate oven for 1 hour or until tender. Cool.
To microwave:
Combine meat, kidneys, seasoned flour, nutmeg, thyme, onion, stock, bay leaf and Worcestershire sauce in a microwave-safe dish. Cover and cook on high (100% power) for 10 minutes. Reduce to 50% and cook 15–20 minutes or until tender. Cool.

2. Roll out pastry 2.5cm/1in. larger than top of pie dish. Cut off a 1cm/½in. strip from round the edge of the pastry and put round the dampened rim of the dish.
3. Cover dish with pastry. Press edges firmly; trim. Glaze with beaten egg.
4. Bake in a hot oven for 20–30 minutes or until pastry is golden.

Total preparation and cooking time: 90 minutes

This recipe can be prepared in advance. Top with pastry, refrigerate and bake the following day.

PASTRY TIP
Always leave glazing of pastry until immediately before baking.

Hawaiian Pork Pie

500g/1lb diced pork
2–3 tablespoons flour
1 tablespoon oil
1 medium onion, finely sliced
2 tablespoons tomato paste (purée)
½ cup/90g/3oz. sultanas
410g/13oz. can unsweetened pineapple pieces, undrained
¼ cup/60ml/2fl. oz. water
1 teaspoon Worcestershire sauce
salt and pepper to taste
1 sheet puff pastry, thawed
beaten egg for glazing

SERVES 4–6

1. Lightly coat pork with flour. Heat oil, add onion and pork, and cook until pork is lightly browned. Remove from heat.
2. Add tomato paste, sultanas, pineapple, reserved liquid, water, and Worcestershire sauce to the pan. Season with salt and pepper. Return to the heat, bring to the boil, then reduce heat and simmer until meat is tender (approximately 50 minutes). Cool.
3. Roll out pastry thinly. Spoon mixture into a 1-litre/1¾-pint pie dish. Cover dish with pastry; trim edges. Decorate sides with a knife and top with pastry leaves if desired.
4. Brush pastry top with beaten egg. Bake in a hot oven for 20 minutes or until golden brown.

Total preparation and cooking time: 90 minutes

The filling can be made in advance, and refrigerated or frozen. When required, it can be topped with pastry and baked.

Curried Lamb Casserole
Quiche Lorraine
Chicken Pastie
Recipes, page 28

Quiche Lorraine

185g/6oz. shortcrust pastry, thawed
½ cup/30g/1oz. mushrooms, sliced
½ cup/60g/2oz. ham, finely chopped
½ cup/125g/4oz. grated cheese
1 cup/250ml/8fl. oz. cream
2 eggs
2 egg yolks

SERVES 6–8

1. Roll out pastry and use to line a deep
20cm/8in. flan tin. Bake 'blind' in a moderately
hot oven for 10–15 minutes.
2. Arrange mushrooms, ham and cheese in
base of pastry case.
3. Combine cream, eggs, egg yolk and seasoning.
Mix well. Pour egg mixture carefully over
ingredients in pastry case.
4. Bake in a moderate oven for 30–35 minutes
or until set.

Total preparation and cooking time: 50 minutes

This recipe does not freeze.

Curried Lamb Casserole

Tops for dinner

750g/1½lb lamb shoulder meat, diced
2 tablespoons flour
2–3 tablespoons vegetable oil
2 cloves garlic, crushed
1 large onion, sliced
2–3 teaspoons curry powder
1 teaspoon grated fresh ginger
2 cups/250g/8oz. chopped vegetables
(carrots, celery, parsnip, etc.)
2 bay leaves
1 cup/250ml/8fl. oz. stock (stock cubes and water)
2 sheets puff pastry, thawed
½ cup/20g/⅔oz. fresh coriander or
½ teaspoon dried coriander
beaten egg for glazing

SERVES 4–6

1. Toss cubed meat in flour to coat lightly.
Sauté in heated oil until browned all over.
Remove and set aside.
2. Add garlic, onion and curry powder to the
pan and fry gently, stirring well, for 1–2 minutes.
Stir in ginger and vegetables, and cook 1–2 minutes
longer.
3. Return meat to the pan and add bay
leaves and stock, stir well, cover, and simmer
25–30 minutes until meat and vegetables are
tender. Cool.

4. Roll out pastry 2.5cm/1in. larger than top of
1-litre/1¾-pint casserole dish. Cut off a 1cm/½in.
strip from round the edge of the pastry. Place
around rim of casserole dish and lightly brush
with water. Place a pie funnel in centre of dish.
5. Spoon lamb mixture into casserole dish.
Sprinkle with coriander. Make a crosswise slit in
centre of pastry; cover dish with the pastry. Press
edges firmly, and trim.
6. Brush pastry top with beaten egg. Bake in
a hot oven for 30–35 minutes or until golden
brown. Serve immediately.

Total preparation and cooking time: 90 minutes

*The filling can be made in advance, and refrigerated
or frozen. When required, top with puff pastry and bake.*

PASTRY TIP

Pie funnels or pie birds are functional, useful
and fun when making pies with a pastry lid
only. Their function is to allow the steam to
escape from underneath the crust, through their
open beak protruding from the pastry lid. In
addition, a pie funnel or pie bird, or even an
inverted china egg-cup, has another practical
and aesthetic use: it helps to support the centre
portion of the pastry, especially if the meat or
fruit shrinks during baking, resulting in a well-
baked, browned, attractive pie crust.

Chicken Pasties

What's for lunch?

4 chicken fillets, skin removed
8 dried apricots, sliced
1 tablespoon raisins
2 tablespoons chopped almonds
2 tablespoons chopped fresh parsley
¼ cup/30g/1oz. grated cheese
500g/1lb puff pastry, thawed
beaten egg for glazing

SERVES 4

1. Flatten chicken fillets, using a rolling pin or
the flat side of a meat mallet.
2. Combine apricots, raisins, almonds, parsley
and cheese. Divide the apricot mixture evenly
between the chicken fillets. Fold the chicken
around the filling.
3. Cut pastry into 4 and roll out each portion
to a 23cm/9in. square. Place a chicken fillet on
each pastry piece, fold in half to form a pastie
shape, trim edges and crimp with a fork. Use
pastry scraps for decoration.

Savoury Beef Roll

4. Glaze; cut a vent in centre of pastie tops.
5. Bake in a moderately hot oven for 25–30 minutes or until pastry is golden brown.

Total preparation and cooking time: 50 minutes

These pasties freeze well. Prepare up to the cooking stage, then freeze. Cook from frozen on the day they are required, adding 10 minutes to cooking time.

Savoury Beef Roll

Serve one, freeze one

500g/1lb lean minced beef
1½ cups/90g/3oz. fresh breadcrumbs
1 onion, finely chopped
½ cup/60g/2oz. grated carrot
½ green capsicum (pepper), finely chopped
½ cup/60g/2oz. finely chopped celery
2 beef stock cubes
1 tablespoon Worcestershire sauce
3 tablespoons tomato paste (purée)
½ teaspoon lemon pepper
2 tablespoons chopped fresh parsley
500g/1lb puff pastry, thawed
beaten egg for glazing

SERVES 4–8 (MAKES TWO ROLLS)

1. Combine beef, breadcrumbs, vegetables, beef stock cubes, Worcestershire sauce, tomato paste, pepper and parsley. Mix well.
2. Cut pastry into 2 and roll out each piece to a 30cm/12in. square. Spoon half the meat mixture into the centre of one piece of pastry, forming mixture into a log shape.
3. Brush edges of pastry lightly with water, fold sides up on top of meat and seal edges. Tuck ends under. Repeat with remaining pastry and meat.
4. Place rolls on a baking sheet; glaze. Bake in a hot oven 30–35 minutes or until golden brown.

Total preparation and cooking time: 50 minutes

This recipe freezes well. Make the rolls up to the baking stage; wrap in freezer wrap and store in the freezer. Bake from frozen, increasing baking time to 45–50 minutes.

Fish Pie

A delicious catch

500g/1lb white fish fillets, diced and
coated with flour
1 red onion, sliced
3 medium-size ripe tomatoes, roughly chopped
2 cups/315g/10oz. frozen mixed vegetables
2 tablespoons tomato paste (purée)
1 teaspoon dried dill
rind from 1 lemon, peeled and finely chopped
185g/6oz. puff pastry, thawed
beaten egg for glazing

SERVES 4–6

1. Combine first 7 ingredients and place in a
lightly greased 2-litre/3½-pint casserole dish.
Place a pie funnel in centre.
2. Roll out pastry 2.5cm/1in. larger than dish.
Cut off a 1cm/½in. strip from round edge of
pastry, place around rim of dish and lightly
brush with water.
3. Make a crosswise slit in centre of pastry.
Cover dish with puff pastry. Press edges firmly,
and trim.
4. Brush pastry top with beaten egg. Bake in
a hot oven for 30–35 minutes or until golden
brown. Serve immediately with fresh vegetables
or salad.

Total preparation and cooking time: 50 minutes

This recipe does not freeze.

Cornish Plait

1 medium potato
1 small carrot
1 small onion
¼ white turnip
250g/8oz. lean minced beef
ground black pepper
1 tablespoon Worcestershire sauce
185g/6oz. shortcrust pastry, thawed
beaten egg for glazing

SERVES 4–6

1. Peel and finely dice vegetables. Combine
vegetables with meat and seasonings; mix well.
2. Roll out pastry thinly to a large oblong.
Place pastry on a lightly greased baking sheet.
3. Spoon meat and vegetable mixture down
centre of pastry, forming mixture into a log
shape. Brush edges of pastry lightly with water.

On either side of filling, make diagonal cuts at
1cm/½in. intervals, to produce 1cm/½in.-wide
pastry strips. Lift alternate strips over filling, to
make a plait. Glaze with beaten egg.
4. Bake in a moderately hot oven for 50 minutes
or until pastry is golden brown. Serve hot or cold.

Total preparation and cooking time: 70 minutes

This recipe freezes well.

Minced Meat Pies

1 onion, finely chopped
500g/1lb lean minced beef
1 cup/250ml/8fl. oz. water
2 beef stock cubes, crumbled
¼ cup/60ml/2fl. oz. tomato sauce
2 teaspoons Worcestershire sauce
pepper to taste
½ teaspoon ground oregano
pinch nutmeg
3 tablespoons plain flour
125g/4oz. shortcrust pastry, thawed
125g/4oz. puff pastry, thawed
beaten egg for glazing

SERVES 4

1. Cook onion and meat until meat is well
browned. Add ¾ cup/185ml/6fl. oz. water, stock
cubes, sauces and seasonings, bring to the boil,
cover, and simmer 15 minutes.
2. Blend flour with remaining water to make a
smooth paste. Add to the meat and bring to the
boil, stirring continuously; boil 5 minutes. Cool.
3. Roll out shortcrust pastry thinly and line a
lightly greased pie plate or individual dishes.
4. Spoon in the cooled meat filling.
5. Roll out puff pastry thinly. Moisten edges
of pastry base with water. Top with puff pastry,
pressing down gently to seal edges. Trim and
score edges. Glaze.
6. Bake in a very hot oven for 15 minutes,
reduce to moderately hot and cook a further
25 minutes or until pastry is golden.
N.B.: For individual pies, 250g/8oz. of each
pastry will be required.

Total preparation and cooking time: 90 minutes

*These pies freeze well. Prepare up to the baking
stage, then freeze. Cook from frozen on the day they
are required.*

Cheese & Vegetable Pie

250g/8oz. shortcrust pastry, thawed
2½ cups/500g/1lb broccoli florets
1 carrot, peeled and sliced
1 small potato, peeled and sliced
1 cup/125g/4oz. sliced celery
1 small onion, sliced
1 cup/60g/2oz. sliced mushrooms
4 eggs
1 cup/125g/4oz. grated cheese
½ cup/125ml/4fl. oz. milk
2 tablespoons chopped fresh parsley

SERVES 6

1. Roll out pastry thinly and line a deep 20cm/8in. pie plate.
2. Blanch broccoli, carrot and potato, or microwave on high (100% power) for 2–3 minutes.
3. Layer all vegetables in pastry-lined pie plate.
4. Combine eggs, cheese, milk and parsley. Mix well. Carefully pour egg mixture over vegetables.
5. Bake in a moderate oven for 55–60 minutes or until custard is set. Serve hot or cold.

Total preparation and cooking time: 90 minutes

This recipe does not freeze.

PASTRY TIP

For better cooking results, use a dull, dark metal dish or sheet for baking.

Spinach Pie

1 bunch spinach or silverbeet
1 teaspoon salt
6 shallots or spring onions, chopped
1 tablespoon polyunsaturated oil
5 eggs
250g/8oz. fetta cheese
250g/8oz. grated cheese
¼ cup/30g/1oz. grated parmesan cheese
¼ cup/15g/½oz. chopped fresh parsley
¼ teaspoon black pepper
1/8 teaspoon grated nutmeg
280g/9oz. filo pastry, thawed
1/3 cup/75ml/2½fl. oz. polyunsaturated oil

SERVES 8–10

Cheese & Vegetable Pie

Spinach Pie

1. Wash spinach or silverbeet in water until all traces of grit are removed. Trim leaves from the stalks.

2. Chop leaves roughly, place in a colander, sprinkle with salt and allow to stand for 1 hour. Drain and press out as much liquid as possible.

3. Sauté chopped shallots or spring onions in 1 tablespoon oil for 5 minutes, or microwave on high (100% power) for 1 minute.

4. Combine eggs, cheeses, shallots or spring onions, spinach or silverbeet, parsley and seasonings. Mix well.

5. Separate pastry and brush half the sheets with oil; layer. Use to line the base and sides of a medium-size (23cm x 18cm x 5cm/9in. x 7in. x 2in.) baking dish.

6. Spoon in filling and spread evenly.

7. Brush remaining pastry with oil, and layer; use to cover filling. Neaten edges of pastry by folding over. Brush top with oil. With a sharp knife, score pastry diagonally to make diamond-shaped pieces.

8. Bake in a moderate oven for 30–40 minutes or until pastry is golden. Serve hot or cold.

Total preparation and cooking time: 1 hour 40 minutes

This recipe can be frozen unbaked. Cook from frozen when it is required. Extend the cooking time to 50–60 minutes.

Main Meal Bolognese Pizza

A taste of Italy

1 tablespoon oil
1 clove garlic, crushed
1 onion, chopped
250g/8oz. lean minced beef
410g/13oz. can tomatoes, chopped
¼ cup/60ml/2fl. oz. juice from tomatoes
2 tablespoons tomato paste (purée)
100g/3½oz. mushrooms, sliced
½ teaspoon each dried thyme and oregano
2 ready-made pizza bases
1 red capsicum (pepper), sliced
1 cup/125g/4oz. grated mozzarella cheese

SERVES 6

1. Heat oil, add garlic and onion, and cook for 2–3 minutes. Add meat and cook, stirring continuously, until meat is evenly browned. Add tomatoes, juice, tomato paste, mushrooms and seasonings. Bring to the boil; simmer for 5 minutes.

2. Place 1 pizza base on a pizza or baking sheet. Spread with meat sauce to within 1cm/½in. of edge; top with capsicum and half the cheese. Place second pizza base on top, pressing down lightly. Sprinkle with remaining cheese.

3. Bake in a hot oven for 15–20 minutes or until cheese is golden and base of pizza is cooked through. Serve as a main meal with a crisp tossed salad.

Total preparation and cooking time: 30 minutes

This recipe does not freeze.

Main Meal Bolognese Pizza

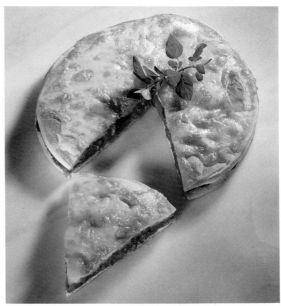

Vanilla Slices

From your home patisserie

2 sheets puff pastry, thawed
⅓ cup/45g/1½oz. custard powder
½ cup /125g/4oz. caster sugar
600ml/1 pint milk
1 tablespoon gelatine
⅓ cup/75ml/2½fl. oz. hot water
1 teaspoon vanilla essence
300ml/10fl. oz. double cream
icing sugar

MAKES 16

1. Roll out each pastry sheet to a 25cm/10in. square. Place pastry on ungreased baking sheets; prick well with a fork. Bake in a very hot oven for 5–10 minutes or until puffed and golden. While still warm, trim pastry with a sharp knife to a 23cm/9in. square.
2. Blend custard powder and sugar with sufficient milk to form a smooth paste; add remaining milk. Cook over low heat, stirring constantly, until mixture boils and thickens. Cook for 1 minute; remove from heat.
3. Sprinkle gelatine onto hot water; stir briskly until thoroughly dissolved. Stir into custard. Place a piece of dampened greaseproof or plastic wrap flat down on the custard (this prevents a skin from forming). Allow to cool.
4. Add vanilla. Gradually add cream, beating at high speed until well blended.
5. Line sides and base of a 23cm/9in. square cake pan with a strip of foil. Place one sheet of cooked pastry on base; pour custard onto base; top with remaining sheet of cooked pastry, pressing down firmly.
6. Dust liberally with icing sugar. Refrigerate for 6 hours or overnight. Cut into squares.

Total preparation and cooking time: 40 minutes

Variation: *Chocolate*

Blend ⅓–½ cup/45–60g/1½–2oz. cocoa with custard powder.

Variation: *Mocha Rum*

Dissolve 1 tablespoon powdered instant coffee and ⅓ cup/45g/1½oz. cocoa with gelatine. Add 2 tablespoons dark rum.

This recipe does not freeze.

Vanilla Slices
Lemon Meringue Tart
Recipe, page 36

Lemon Meringue Tart

Sweet endings

185g/6oz. shortcrust pastry, thawed
4 tablespoons cornflour
300ml/10fl. oz. water
30g/1oz. butter or margarine
juice of 3 lemons (½ cup/125ml/4fl. oz.)
3 teaspoons finely grated lemon rind
1¼ cups/375g/12oz. caster sugar
3 eggs, separated

SERVES 4–6

1. Roll out pastry and use to line a lightly greased 20cm/8in. pie plate, trim edges, crimp, and bake 'blind' in a moderately hot oven for 10 minutes. Remove paper and baking beans and continue to cook pastry a further 10 minutes. Cool.
2. In a saucepan or microwave-safe jug, blend cornflour with sufficient water to form a smooth paste. Add remaining water, butter or margarine, lemon juice, rind and 1 cup/250g/8oz. of sugar. Cook over a low heat, stirring constantly, or microwave on high (100% power), stirring occasionally, until mixture boils and thickens.
3. Remove from heat and cool slightly. Add egg yolks, beating well.
4. Pour into pre-baked pastry case.
5. Beat egg whites until stiff. Gradually add remaining ¼ cup/60g/2oz. sugar, beating constantly until sugar has dissolved (2–3 minutes).
6. Spoon meringue onto lemon filling, making sure that there are no gaps at the edge of the pie plate.
7. Return to the oven and bake until lightly browned – 15–20 minutes – or brown under a medium grill. Serve warm or cold.

Total preparation and cooking time: 50 minutes

This recipe does not freeze.

Pear Normandy

Pass the cream

250g/8oz. shortcrust pastry, thawed
375g/12oz. packet vanilla cake mix
½ cup/60g/2oz. ground hazelnuts
1 pear, peeled, quartered and cut into eighths
icing sugar
whipped cream

SERVES 6–8

1. Roll out pastry and use to line a 23cm/9in. flat tin. Bake 'blind'* in a moderately hot oven for 15 minutes.
2. Make up cake mix as directed on packet, but use only ½ cup/125ml/4fl. oz. liquid and fold in hazelnuts. Pour prepared cake mix into the pastry case.
3. Arrange pears evenly over the cake mix, pressing in lightly. Bake in a moderate oven for 25–30 minutes or until testing shows that cake is cooked. Serve cake warm, dusted with icing sugar. Serve whipped cream separately.

Total preparation and cooking time: 60 minutes

This recipe freezes well.

PASTRY TIP

*To bake 'blind': Line the pastry-lined flan tin with 2 thicknesses of lightly greased greaseproof or brown paper or with foil, extending the paper or foil well up the sides. Fill the base with dried beans or peas, pasta or rice (the 'loading'), gently pushing up the sides.

Custard Tart

185g/6oz. shortcrust pastry, thawed
3 eggs
2 tablespoons sugar
1 teaspoon vanilla essence
2 cups/500ml/16fl. oz. milk
grated nutmeg

SERVES 6–8

1. Roll out pastry and use to line a lightly greased 20cm/8in. pie plate; trim edges, then crimp. Bake 'blind' in a moderately hot oven for 10 minutes. Remove from oven.
2. Beat together eggs, sugar and vanilla until light and fluffy.
3. Heat milk in a saucepan over a low heat until lukewarm. Pour over egg mixture, beating well. Strain.
4. Carefully pour into prepared pastry case. Sprinkle lightly with nutmeg.
5. Bake in a moderate oven for 35–40 minutes or until custard is firm. Serve warm or cold.

Total preparation and cooking time: 60 minutes

Variations: *Apricot* or *Peach Tart*

1. Line pastry case with well-drained contents of a 410g/13oz. can apricots or peaches (sliced or halved). Make up custard as above. Bake as directed.

This recipe does not freeze.

Pecan Pie

Pecan Pie

250g/8oz. shortcrust pastry, thawed
2 eggs
1 cup/185g/6oz. brown sugar
¼ cup/60ml/2fl. oz. golden syrup
45g/1½oz. butter or margarine, melted
1 teaspoon vanilla essence
2 tablespoons plain flour
1¾ cups/250g/8oz. pecans

SERVES 6–8

1. Roll out pastry and use to line a shallow 23cm/9in. flan tin. Bake 'blind' in a moderately hot oven for 10 minutes, remove paper and baking beans, and cook a further 5 minutes. Reduce oven to moderate.
2. Combine eggs, brown sugar, golden syrup, butter or margarine, vanilla, flour and pecans. Mix well.
3. Carefully pour pecan mixture into partly baked pastry case. Return to oven for a further 20 minutes or until filling has set. Serve at room temperature.

Total preparation and cooking time: 45 minutes

This recipe does not freeze.

Apricot Pie

Apricot Pie

500g/1lb puff pastry, thawed
8 creamed vanilla wafer biscuits, crushed
375g/12oz. very ripe apricots, stones removed, *or* 815g/1lb 10oz. can apricot halves, well drained
beaten egg for glazing
2 tablespoons apricot conserve, heated
½ cup/60g/2oz. slivered almonds, toasted

SERVES 6

1. Cut pastry into 2 pieces and roll out one piece to an oblong 33cm x 25cm/13in. x 10in. and the other to 30cm x 23cm/12in. x 9in. Place the smaller piece on a lightly greased baking sheet.
2. Sprinkle the crushed wafers over the pastry, leaving a 2cm/¾in. border.
3. Arrange apricots over the biscuits. Brush pastry edges lightly with water. Place remaining piece of pastry on top, pressing down edges to seal. Glaze.
4. Cut a vent in centre of pastry and score top.
5. Bake in a very hot oven for 15–20 minutes or until pastry is golden.
6. While still hot, brush top of pie with hot apricot conserve and sprinkle with almonds.

Total preparation and cooking time: 35 minutes

This recipe does not freeze.

Honeyed Apple Strudel

810g/1lb 10oz. can unsweetened apples
½ cup/90g/3oz. sultanas
2 tablespoons finely chopped almonds
½ cup/60g/2oz. wholemeal breadcrumbs
1 teaspoon cinnamon
¼ cup/90g/3oz. honey, warmed
10 sheets filo pastry, thawed
2 teaspoons polyunsaturated oil

SERVES 6

1. In a bowl combine apples, sultanas, almonds, breadcrumbs, cinnamon and honey. Mix well.
2. Brush every second sheet of pastry lightly with oil; layer. Spoon apple filling down centre of pastry, leaving a 10cm/4in. border at each end of pastry.

3. Tuck ends in and fold the pastry over filling to make a roll. Place roll seam-side down on an ungreased baking sheet. Brush lightly with oil. With a sharp knife make deep diagonal slits across pastry top.
4. Bake in a moderately hot oven for 30–35 minutes or until golden brown. Serve immediately.

Total preparation and cooking time: 45 minutes

This recipe does not freeze.

PASTRY TIP

Carefully remove the number of sheets of filo pastry required for your recipe. Immediately rewrap the unused pastry in the film, place in a freezer bag and seal for future use. Return to the freezer or, alternatively, store in the refrigerator. Do not refreeze filo more than once.

Honeyed Apple Strudel

HEALTHY EATING

If you love eating well, but value good health just as much,
the appetising, good-for-you recipes in this section should
be part of your lifestyle. Delicious combinations of vegetables,
fruits, fish, poultry and meat in lightweight pastry, they
enhance the flavours of fitness and good living!

Veal Roll-Ups

Veal Roll-Ups

1½ cups/185g/6oz. grated carrot
½ cup/60g/2oz. finely chopped celery
¼ cup/15g/½oz. finely sliced shallots
or spring onions
¼ cup/45g/1½oz. currants
finely grated rind of 1 lemon
6 veal or pork escalopes, flattened
12 sheets filo pastry, thawed
2 teaspoons polyunsaturated oil

SERVES 6

1. Mix together carrots, celery, shallots or spring onions, currants and lemon rind. Divide mixture evenly between the 6 veal or pork escalopes and roll up.
2. Cut pastry sheets in half. Use 4 half-sheets for each roll-up, and brush every second sheet lightly with oil.
3. Place a veal roll on each pastry stack, roll up, tucking ends in tightly.
4. Lightly brush the rolls with oil and place on a baking tray.

5. Bake in a moderately hot oven for 25–30 minutes or until golden brown. Serve hot with salad or vegetables.

Total preparation and cooking time: 45 minutes

This recipe does not freeze.

PASTRY TIP

For tempting, golden pastry, brush top layer of filo pastry lightly with melted margarine or butter or with polyunsaturated oil.

A rule of thumb is to use at least 5 buttered or oiled sheets if substituting filo pastry for puff or shortcrust in your favourite recipe.

Curried Tuna Slice

Curried Tuna Slice

With delicious Mint Sauce

500g/1lb wholemeal or shortcrust pastry,
thawed
445g/14oz. can tuna in brine, well drained
and flaked
1 cup/185g/6oz. cooked rice
1 cup/155g/5oz. frozen peas
⅓ cup/30g/1oz. chopped shallots or spring onions
½ cup/60g/2oz. finely chopped celery
3 hard-boiled eggs, chopped
½ cup/125g/4oz. cottage cheese
2 teaspoons curry powder
½ teaspoon garam masala
beaten egg for glazing

SERVES 6–8

1. Cut pastry into 2 pieces and roll out half
thinly to line a lightly greased 28cm x 18cm/11in.
x 7in. baking tin.
2. Combine tuna, rice, peas, shallots or spring
onions, celery, eggs, cottage cheese and spices.
Mix well. Spoon mixture into pastry-lined tin,
pressing down well.

3. Roll out remaining pastry and use to cover
the filling, trim edges and crimp. Glaze. Cut a
vent in pastry top.
4. Bake in a moderate oven for 35 minutes or
until golden brown. Serve hot or cold.

Total preparation and cooking time: 60 minutes

This recipe freezes well.

Yoghurt Mint Sauce

To accompany Curried Tuna Slice

1 cup/250ml/8fl. oz. natural yoghurt
1–2 tablespoons lemon juice
1 tablespoon finely chopped fresh mint

1. Combine all ingredients. Serve either cold or
just warm (do not allow mixture to boil).

PASTRY TIP

Wholemeal pastry will add colour and nutrition
to finished baked dishes and is ideal for baking
pies, quiches, flans, tarts, etc.

Mushroom & Courgette Quiche

250g/8oz. wholemeal or shortcrust pastry, thawed
1½ cups/90g/3oz. sliced mushrooms
1 cup/125g/4oz. grated courgettes
1 onion, finely chopped
3 eggs
1 cup/250ml/8fl. oz. milk
1 cup/125g/4oz. grated cheese
2 tablespoons finely chopped fresh parsley
1 teaspoon dried thyme
ground black pepper

SERVES 6–8

1. Roll out pastry and use to line a lightly greased, deep 20cm/8in. fluted flan tin with pastry; trim edges. Bake 'blind' in a moderately hot oven for 15 minutes.
2. Combine mushrooms, courgettes and onion. Place in the prepared pastry case. Beat together eggs, milk, ⅔ of the cheese, the parsley and the seasonings. Mix well.
3. Pour egg mixture carefully over ingredients in pastry case. Top with remaining cheese.
4. Bake in a moderate oven for 35–40 minutes or until set. Serve hot or cold.

Total preparation and cooking time: 70 minutes

This recipe does not freeze.

PASTRY TIP

For the preparation of pie bases, quiches, tarts and flans, it is important to choose the correct pastry. We recommend the use of shortcrust pastry or wholemeal pastry, as these pastries can produce a crisp base on pies, tarts, quiches and flans.

Carrot & Fetta Quiche

Great for picnics

8 sheets filo pastry, thawed
2 teaspoons polyunsaturated oil
2 medium carrots, grated
250g/8oz. fetta cheese, crumbled
2 rashers bacon, chopped
¼ cup/15g/½oz. chopped shallots or spring onions
3 eggs
½ cup/125ml/4fl. oz. evaporated milk
½ teaspoon dried basil
ground black pepper

SERVES 4–6

1. Brush every second sheet of pastry lightly with oil. Layer the pastry in a lightly greased, deep 20cm/8in. fluted quiche dish.
2. Arrange carrot, cheese, bacon and shallots or spring onions in the pastry case. Beat together eggs, milk, basil and pepper. Carefully pour the egg mixture over ingredients in pastry case.
3. Bake in a moderate oven for 60 minutes or until mixture is set. Serve hot or cold.

Total preparation and cooking time: 80 minutes

This recipe does not freeze.

Chicken & Fruit Parcels

Tuck in!

6 chicken fillets
½ cup/60g/2oz. flour
90g/3oz. butter or margarine
12 sheets filo pastry, thawed
2 tablespoons finely chopped fresh mint
300g/10oz. fresh or canned apricots or peaches, well drained and sliced
sesame seeds

SERVES 6

1. Lightly coat each chicken fillet with flour. Melt 30g/1oz. of butter or margarine in a frying pan, add chicken and cook until brown on both sides. Remove from pan and drain. Cool.
2. Melt remaining butter. Take 2 sheets of pastry and brush each sheet with the melted butter or margarine. Layer the 2 sheets, then fold in half. Repeat with remaining pastry.
3. Make an incision in the centre of each chicken fillet; fill each cavity with mint and apricots or peaches. Place a chicken fillet on each folded sheet of pastry. Roll chicken up in pastry, folding in the sides to form a parcel.
4. Place on an ungreased baking sheet, seam-side down, and brush top with melted butter or margarine. Sprinkle with sesame seeds.
5. Bake in a moderate oven for 30 minutes or until golden brown. Serve hot with vegetables or salad.

Total preparation and cooking time: 50 minutes

This recipe does not freeze.

Carrot & Fetta Quiche

Chicken in Filo Nest

Spinach & Cottage Cheese Pie

1 bunch spinach, washed and coarsely chopped
¼ cup/15g/½oz. chopped shallots or spring onions
250g/8oz. low-fat cottage cheese
1 egg
ground black pepper
6 sheets filo pastry, thawed
2 teaspoons polyunsaturated oil

SERVES 4–6

1. Place spinach and shallots or spring onions in a saucepan. Cover and cook over gentle heat until spinach is tender. Drain spinach well. Allow to cool then chop finely.
2. Combine spinach mixture, cottage cheese, egg and black pepper; mix well.
3. Brush every second sheet of pastry lightly with oil. Layer the pastry in a shallow 20cm/8in. square cake tin; push pastry gently into corners. Spoon spinach mixture into pastry. Fold pastry edges over the spinach filling. Brush top lightly with oil.
4. Bake in a moderately hot oven for 30–35 minutes or until golden brown. Serve immediately.

Total preparation and cooking time: 50 minutes

This recipe does not freeze.

PASTRY TIP

Always place the pastry dish in the centre of the oven or at the one-below centre shelf position in the oven. This allows more heat concentration on the bottom crust.

Chicken in Filo Nests

For health watchers

9 sheets filo pastry, thawed
2 teaspoons polyunsaturated oil
2 cups/250g/8oz. cooked, chopped chicken
¼ cup/15g/½oz. chopped shallots or spring onions
1 cup/60g/2oz. sliced mushrooms
½ cup/60g/2oz. sliced celery
250ml/8fl. oz. light sour cream or yoghurt
3 eggs
ground black pepper

SERVES 4–6 (makes 9 nests)

1. Cut pastry sheets in half lengthwise and then cut each half into 3 pieces. Use 6 pieces of pastry for each nest; lightly brush every second sheet with oil, and layer.
2. Place prepared pastry stacks in 9, 9cm/3½in. muffin tins or deep patty tins. Press in gently.
3. Combine chicken, shallots or spring onions, mushrooms, celery, sour cream, eggs and seasonings. Mix well.
4. Spoon chicken mixture into the pastry-lined cases. Bake in a moderate oven for 30–35 minutes or until filling is set. Serve hot or cold.

Total preparation and cooking time: 60 minutes

This recipe does not freeze.

PASTRY TIP

Muffin tins are great for individual serves of all types of pies and savouries.

Quick & Light Seafood Baskets

375g/12oz. white fish fillets, cut into cubes
3 tablespoons finely chopped shallots or spring onions
2 tablespoons pine nuts
½ cup/30g/1oz. fresh breadcrumbs
¾ cup/185ml/6fl. oz. natural yoghurt
1 teaspoon finely grated lemon rind
2 teaspoons finely chopped fresh chives
6 sheets filo pastry, thawed
2 teaspoons polyunsaturated oil

SERVES 4

1. Combine fish, shallots or spring onions, pine nuts, breadcrumbs, yoghurt, lemon rind and chives.

Quick & Light Seafood Baskets

2. Lightly brush every second sheet of pastry with oil; layer. Cut pastry into 4 and place in four 10cm/4in. flan tins.
3. Spoon fish mixture into pastry-lined cases. Bake in a moderate oven for 10–15 minutes or until fish is opaque and pastry is golden.

Total preparation and cooking time: 45 minutes

This recipe does not freeze.

PASTRY TIP

Pastry always cooks better in dark, dull metal dishes. Ceramic dishes are not ideal for cooking pastry bases, as they are poor conductors of heat and will not give a crisp result.

Pork with Prunes & Apples

15g/½oz. butter or margarine
¼ cup/15g/½oz. chopped shallots or spring onions
1 large apple, peeled, cored and finely chopped
¼ cup/30g/1oz. prunes, seeded and chopped
2 pork fillets
8 sheets filo pastry, thawed
2 teaspoons polyunsaturated oil

SERVES 4

1. Melt half the butter or margarine. Add shallots or spring onions, and apple; cook until tender. Combine with prunes.
2. Cut each pork fillet into 2 pieces, cut a pocket in each piece and fill with the apple mixture. Close pocket; secure with skewers if necessary.

3. Heat remaining butter or margarine and seal the pork on all sides over moderate heat. Cool.
4. Cut pastry in half widthwise. Use 4 pieces of pastry for each serving, brush every second piece of pastry lightly with oil, and layer.
5. Place a prepared piece of pork on each stack of pastry. Roll up, and press the ends together to seal.
6. Place on a lightly greased baking sheet; brush with oil. Bake in a moderately hot oven for 25–30 minutes or until golden brown. Serve hot with freshly cooked vegetables, accompanied by hot apple sauce.

Total preparation and cooking time: 60 minutes

This recipe does not freeze.

PASTRY TIP

Allow frozen filo pastry to completely thaw in the plastic bag, in or out of the outer packaging, at room temperature for approximately 2 hours. Alternatively, allow filo to thaw overnight in the refrigerator and for 1 hour at room temperature. Do not use heat to accelerate thawing. Pastry should not be thawed in a microwave oven.

Hot Apple Sauce

a knob of butter or margarine
1 tablespoon chopped shallots or spring onions
1 cup/315g/10oz. apple purée (fresh apple slices or canned)
3 tablespoons water
1 tablespoon brown sugar
2 teaspoons lemon juice
freshly ground black pepper

1. Melt butter or margarine, add shallots or spring onions and cook for 1 minute. Stir in remaining ingredients and cook, stirring occasionally, until heated through.

PASTRY TIP

Basically filo pastry works on the same principle as puff pastry. This is why it is imperative that melted butter or margarine and/or edible oil be brushed on each or alternate sheets before layering. While the filo bakes, steam separates the sheets and then the buttering between the sheets fries each thin layer of dough individually and makes each one crispy and flaky.

Seafood Casserole

Great catch

15g/½oz. butter or margarine
1 onion, finely chopped
1 clove garlic, crushed
440g/14oz. can tomatoes
2 tablespoons tomato paste (purée)
½ medium red capsicum (pepper), sliced
¼ cup/60ml/2fl. oz. dry white wine
1 teaspoon each dried oregano and thyme
ground black pepper
500g/1lb raw, peeled prawns
250g/8oz. white fish fillets, cut into cubes
100g/3½oz. calamari (squid) rings
6 sheets filo pastry, thawed
2 teaspoons polyunsaturated oil

SERVES 6–8

1. Melt butter or margarine. Add onion and garlic; cook 1 minute. Stir in tomatoes and juice from can, tomato paste, capsicum, wine and seasoning. Cook for 5 minutes. Add prepared seafood and cook a further 5 minutes. Cool.
2. Place tomato and seafood mixture in an ovenproof serving dish.
3. Brush every second sheet of pastry lightly with oil, and layer. Carefully pleat pastry to fit the top of the dish.
4. Bake in a moderately hot oven for 25–30 minutes or until pastry is golden brown. Serve hot with salad.

Total preparation and cooking time: 70 minutes

This recipe does not freeze.

PASTRY TIP

Wrap unused filo pastry sheets in 6–8-sheet lots for convenient re-use. Remember: it can be refrozen *once*.

Seafood Casserole
Savoury Pumpkin and Leek Tart
Wholemeal Date Crumble Bars
Recipes, page 48

Savoury Pumpkin & Leek Tart

250g/8oz. wholemeal or shortcrust pastry, thawed
15g/½oz. butter or margarine
1 cup/125g/4oz. sliced leeks, well washed
1.5kg/3lb pumpkin, peeled, cooked, drained
and mashed
1 tablespoon chopped fresh chives
3 eggs
1 tablespoon plain flour
pinch nutmeg and black pepper

SERVES 6–8

1. Line a lightly greased, deep 20cm/8in. fluted flan tin with pastry; trim edges. Bake 'blind' in a moderately hot oven for 15 minutes.
2. Melt butter or margarine, add leeks and cook until tender.
3. Combine cooked leeks, pumpkin, chives, eggs, flour and seasoning. Mix well.
4. Spoon pumpkin filling into prepared pastry case. Return to oven and cook a further 30–40 minutes or until filling is set.
5. Serve hot or cold with a crisp salad.

Total preparation and cooking time: 70 minutes

This recipe does not freeze.

PASTRY TIP

Once baked, always place the pastry dish on a wire cake rack. This allows air to flow around the dish and prevents condensation on the pastry base.

Wholemeal Date Crumble Bars

2 cups/315g/10oz. chopped dates
1 cup/250ml/8fl. oz. water
125g/4oz. wholemeal or shortcrust pastry, thawed
½ cup/45g/1½oz. desiccated coconut
½ cup/60g/2oz. self-raising flour
¼ cup/45g/1½oz. rolled oats
¼ cup/45g/1½oz. brown sugar
30g/1oz. butter or margarine
lemon icing

MAKES 24 SMALL BARS

1. Place dates and water in a small saucepan. Cook over gentle heat until mixture is thick and water has been absorbed. Alternatively, microwave on high (100% power) for 5 minutes. Cool.
2. Roll out pastry to an 28cm x 20cm/11in. x 8in. oblong, then place on lightly greased baking sheet. Spread the cold date mixture evenly over pastry, going as close to the edge as possible.
3. Combine coconut, flour, oats, sugar, and butter or margarine. Rub in with fingertips until mixture is well moistened. Sprinkle crumble mixture evenly over dates, pressing in lightly.
4. Bake in a moderately hot oven for 12–15 minutes or until pastry is cooked through. Cool. Drizzle with lemon icing. Cut into fingers and store when cold.

Total preparation and cooking time: 30 minutes

This recipe does not freeze.

Deep Dish Family Apple Pie

250g/8oz. shortcrust pastry, thawed
7 large Granny Smith apples, peeled and sliced
60g/2oz. sugar
4 cloves
1 teaspoon finely grated lemon rind
beaten egg for glazing

SERVES 8

1. Roll out pastry and use to line a deep 24cm/9½in. flan tin. Bake 'blind' in a moderately hot oven for 15 minutes. Carefully remove greaseproof paper and baking beans.
2. Place apples, sugar, cloves and lemon rind in a large saucepan; cook until tender. Cool then drain off any excess liquid.
To microwave:
Place apples, sugar, cloves and lemon rind in a microwave-safe dish; cover. Microwave on high (100% power) for 10–12 minutes or until tender. Cool and drain.
3. Layer apple into prepared pastry case. Use pastry trimmings to cover pie. Cut circles, using 3 different-sized cutters. Use the larger circles around the outside and the smallest on the inside. Glaze with beaten egg.
4. Bake in a moderate oven for 35–40 minutes or until golden. Serve hot.

Total preparation and cooking time: 80 minutes

This recipe does not freeze.

Deep Dish Family Apple Pie

Creamy Fruit Strudel

Coffee time!

1½ cups/250g/8oz. mixed dried fruits
2 tablespoons lemon juice
¾ cup/185ml/6fl. oz. natural yoghurt
1 cup/250g/8oz. ricotta cheese
¼ cup/30g/1oz. slivered almonds, toasted
¼ teaspoon cinnamon
¼ teaspoon nutmeg
9 sheets filo pastry, thawed
3 teaspoons polyunsaturated oil
¼ cup/15g/½oz. fresh breadcrumbs

SERVES 8–10

1. Combine fruit and lemon juice; allow to stand for 10 minutes. Stir in yoghurt, ricotta, almonds, cinnamon and nutmeg. Mix well.
2. Brush every second sheet of pastry lightly with oil and sprinkle evenly with breadcrumbs. Layer.

3. Spoon fruit mixture down the centre of pastry, leaving a 4cm/1¾in. border at each end. Fold pastry edges into the centre, over filling, tuck ends in and fold the pastry over filling to make a roll. Place roll seam-side down on an ungreased baking sheet. Brush lightly with oil. With a sharp knife cut diagonal slits across pastry top.
4. Bake in a moderately hot oven for 25–30 minutes or until golden brown.
5. Serve warm or cold.

Total preparation and cooking time: 70 minutes

This recipe does not freeze.

PASTRY TIP

For best results, it is important that you work quickly when layering filo, as drying may occur.

Creamy Fruit Strudel

EASY ENTERTAINING

You'll welcome our special collation of spectacular (but easy!) dishes for hospitable occasions. They have the delectable glamour of stylish international cuisine, but are relatively inexpensive and simple to prepare. These are recipes for success if you are one of those people who love to entertain.

Soup Surprise

15g/½oz. butter or margarine
1 teaspoon curry powder
1 onion, finely chopped
440g/14oz. can chicken consommé
½ large green lettuce, coarsely chopped
2½ cups/375g/12oz. frozen peas
seasoning
2 sheets ready-rolled puff pastry, thawed
egg white
beaten egg for glazing

SERVES 4

1. Melt butter or margarine, add curry powder and onion, and cook for 1–2 minutes. Add consommé, lettuce, peas and seasonings. Simmer until peas are tender. Purée.
To microwave:
Place butter or margarine, curry powder and onion in a large microwave-safe bowl. Cook on high (100% power) for 2–3 minutes. Blend in consommé, lettuce and peas. Cook on high (100% power) for 10–15 minutes or until vegetables are tender. Adjust seasonings. Purée.
2. Roll out pastry thinly and using the soup bowls as a guide, cut 4 pastry shapes to fit the tops of the soup bowls, leaving an extra 1.5cm/¾in. as a border.
3. Pour prepared soup into the 4 serving bowls, until only two-thirds full.
4. Lightly brush the underside of the pastry shapes with egg white. Place pastry over soup and crimp edges. Glaze with beaten egg.
5. Bake in a very hot oven for 10–15 minutes or until pastry is well risen and golden. Serve immediately.

Total preparation and cooking time: 40 minutes

This recipe does not freeze.

Individual Beef Wellingtons

Dinner in London…

15g/½oz. butter or margarine
1 cup/60g/2oz. sliced mushrooms
6 shallots or spring onions, finely chopped
4 thick slices fillet steak
155g/5oz. prepared pâté
4 sheets ready-rolled puff pastry, thawed
beaten egg for glazing

SERVES 4

1. Melt butter or margarine; add mushrooms, and shallots or spring onions. Cook until tender.

Remove from pan. Add the steaks to the pan and seal for 1 minute on each side. Cool.
2. Spread pâté evenly on one side of each slice of steak.
3. Roll out each sheet of pastry to a 23cm/9in. square. Place a spoonful of mushroom mixture in the centre of each sheet of pastry. Top with steak, pâté side down. Wrap up, cutting of excess pastry (use to decorate top). Glaze with beaten egg.
4. Bake in a hot oven for 15–20 minutes or until pastry is golden brown. Serve hot with freshly cooked vegetables.

Total preparation and cooking time: 70 minutes

This recipe does not freeze.

Lamb en Croute

… Lunch in Paris

3 rashers bacon, finely chopped
1 onion, finely chopped
1 cup/125g/4oz. fresh breadcrumbs
2 teaspoons finely chopped fresh rosemary or
1 teaspoon dried rosemary
2 tablespoons chopped fresh parsley
½ teaspoon finely grated lemon rind
1kg/2lb leg of lamb, boned and butterflied
2 teaspoons polyunsaturated oil
500g/1lb puff pastry, thawed
beaten egg for glazing

SERVES 6–8

1. Place bacon and onion in a small pan and cook for 1–2 minutes. Remove from heat and combine with breadcrumbs, rosemary, parsley and lemon rind. Mix well.
2. Place stuffing inside lamb and roll up. Secure with skewers or string. Heat oil in frying pan and seal lamb well on all sides. Cool. Remove skewer or string.
3. Roll out pastry thinly. Place lamb in centre of pastry and wrap up. Place seam-side down on a lightly greased baking sheet. Decorate with extra pastry. Glaze.
4. Bake in a moderately hot oven for 45–50 minutes or until pastry is golden. Serve sliced, with freshly cooked vegetables.

Total preparation and cooking time: 80 minutes

This recipe does not freeze.

Lamb en Croute

Smoked Chicken & Mango Tartlets

Smoked Chicken & Mango Tartlets

6 sheets filo pastry, thawed
2 teaspoons polyunsaturated oil
4 tablespoons mayonnaise
lettuce leaves
8 slices smoked chicken (or turkey)
1 mango, peeled and sliced
4 cherry tomatoes
fresh mint leaves to garnish

SERVES 4

1. Lightly brush every second sheet of pastry with oil, and layer. Cut the oiled stack of pastry into 4 portions.
2. Place pastry in 4 individual tart cases approximately 10cm/4in. in diameter; fold edges under or over to neaten.
3. Bake in a moderate oven for 8–10 minutes. Cool.
4. Carefully spread a small amount of mayonnaise in the base of each tart case, reserving some mayonnaise for garnish. Arrange lettuce leaves, chicken, mango and cherry tomatoes on top of the mayonnaise.
5. Garnish with remaining mayonnaise and mint leaves.

Total preparation and cooking time: 30 minutes

This recipe does not freeze. The tart cases can be made in advance, cooled, and stored in an airtight container until ready to fill.

PASTRY TIP

Filo pastry should never be left uncovered or exposed to room temperature, as the sheets become dried out and difficult to handle. Cover filo pastry, during preparation of a recipe, with plastic wrap or a dry cloth. Do not use a damp cloth because if the cloth is too damp, the moisture in the cloth will transfer to the filo pastry and cause the filo sheets to stick together.

Seafood Nests

30g/1oz. butter or margarine
8 shallots or spring onions
1 small clove garlic, crushed
1 cup/250ml/8fl. oz. dry white wine
300ml/10fl. oz. cream
500g/1lb assorted seafood – prawns, crabmeat, mussels, etc.
2 sheets ready-rolled puff pastry, thawed
beaten egg for glazing

MAKES 8 NESTS

1. Melt butter or margarine; add shallots or spring onions, and garlic. Cook for 2–3 minutes. Add wine and boil rapidly until there is approximately ⅓ cup/75ml/2½fl. oz. of liquid remaining. Add cream and continue to boil until about 1 cup/250ml/8fl. oz. of liquid remains. Add seafood. Cook for 1 minute.
2. Roll out each sheet of pastry to a 23cm/9in. square. Cut each sheet of pastry into 4 squares. Shape each square into a nest by taking the corners and pinching into the centre. Make sure it is secure then fold the lip out. Place on a lightly greased baking sheet. Glaze.
3. Bake in a very hot oven for 10 minutes or until golden brown.
4. Serve the nests filled with the seafood mixture. Serves 4 as a main course and 8 as an entrée.

Total preparation and cooking time: 35 minutes

This recipe does not freeze. The nests can be made, baked, cooled and stored in an airtight container. Reheat in a hot oven for 5 minutes before filling.

Crab Wheel

1 egg, beaten
1 teaspoon Dijon mustard
1 tablespoon chopped fresh chives or parsley
1 cup/125g/4oz. grated Swiss-style cheese
170g/5½oz. can crab meat, drained
(reserve liquid)
1 tablespoon liquid from crab
salt and freshly ground black pepper
2 sheets ready-rolled puff pastry, thawed
1 tablespoon grated parmesan cheese

SERVES 6

1. Beat egg and reserve a little for glazing. Combine remaining egg with mustard, chives or parsley, cheese, crab, liquid from crab, salt and pepper in a bowl and mix together lightly.
2. Roll out each sheet of pastry thinly and cut a 24cm/9½in. circle from each using a plate as a guide. Place sheet on a greased baking sheet.
3. Spread filling on pastry, leaving a 2.5cm/1in. border. Moisten border with water and place second sheet of pastry on top, pressing edges firmly together.*
4. Glaze with beaten egg, sprinkle with parmesan cheese and prick top of pastry with a fork.
5. Bake in a very hot oven for about 15 minutes, until pastry is crisp and golden. Serve as an entrée or main course.
*Edges of pastry can be lifted upwards with the blunt edge of a knife for a decorative effect and good pastry 'lift'.

Total preparation and cooking time: 35 minutes

This recipe does not freeze.

PASTRY TIP

What gives the 'puff' in puff pastry? During baking, the oven temperature converts the water within the pastry to steam. The margarine laminations prevent the steam from escaping and this opens up the layers of dough and margarine. At various temperatures gelatinisation and coagulation, aided by a frying effect of the margarine, sets the dough in this opened or flaky form. This is why a high temperature (very hot, 230°C/450°F), particularly in the first 10 minutes of baking, is important to ensure full extension and that the product sets.

Crab Wheel
Picnic Terrine
Trout & Brie Tartlets
Recipes, page 58

Picnic Terrine

250g/8oz. shortcrust pastry, thawed
500g/1lb pork or veal mince
1 egg
2 tablespoons chopped fresh parsley
1 teaspoon green peppercorns, rinsed
½ cup/60g/2oz. fresh breadcrumbs
1 clove garlic, crushed
2 small chicken fillets, skin removed and sliced
beaten egg for glazing

SERVES 6

1. Roll out three-quarters of the pastry and use to line a 21cm x 10cm/8½in. x 4in. loaf tin, allowing pastry to hang over edges.
2. Combine pork or veal mince, egg, parsley, peppercorns, breadcrumbs and garlic. Mix well.
3. Layer half the meat mixture in the pastry-lined tin. Top with the sliced chicken and remaining meat mixture. Press down firmly.
4. Use remaining pastry to cover top of tin, trim edges and crimp. Cut a vent in top of pastry and decorate with pastry trimmings. Glaze.
5. Bake in a moderate oven for 45 minutes. Allow to cool before removing from tin. Serve at room temperature.

Total preparation and cooking time: 60 minutes

This recipe does not freeze.

Trout & Brie Tartlets

Pour the wine

250g/8oz. shortcrust pastry, thawed
125g/4oz. brie, sliced
100g/3½oz. smoked ocean trout or smoked salmon, sliced
2 tablespoons chopped shallots or spring onions
3 eggs
½ cup/125ml/4fl. oz. cream
¼ teaspoon Dijon mustard
black pepper to taste

SERVES 4

1. Line four 10cm/4in. flan tins with pastry. Bake 'blind' in a moderately hot oven for 15 minutes.
2. Arrange brie, trout or salmon, and shallots or spring onions in the base of the pastry shells.
3. Combine eggs, cream, mustard and black pepper. Mix well. Carefully pour the egg mixture over ingredients in flan tins.

4. Bake in a moderate oven for 20 minutes or until mixture is set. Serve hot or cold.

Total preparation and cooking time: 40 minutes

This recipe does not freeze.

Continental Fruit Ring

3 sheets ready-rolled puff pastry, thawed
beaten egg for glazing
PASTRY CREAM
1½ cups/375ml/12fl. oz. milk
2 eggs
2 egg yolks
2 tablespoons plain flour
¼ cup/60g/2oz. sugar
¼ teaspoon vanilla essence
fresh fruit of your choice

SERVES 6–8

1. Roll out each sheet of pastry thinly and cut a 24cm/9½in. circle from each, using a plate as a guide. Place 1 sheet on a greased baking sheet, brush lightly with water and prick well with a fork.
2. Cut the centre from the two remaining sheets, using a smaller plate, and leaving a 2.5cm/1in. border. Carefully place the pastry frames on the pastry circle. Glaze with beaten egg.
3. Bake in a hot oven for 10–15 minutes or until well risen and golden. Cool.
4. To make Pastry Cream: Heat milk. Beat together eggs, egg yolks, flour and sugar. Gradually add hot milk to the egg mixture. Return to saucepan, and bring to the boil slowly, stirring constantly. Cook 2–3 minutes. Cool; stir in vanilla essence.
5. Place pastry shell on a serving plate. Fill with pastry cream. Garnish with fresh fruit.

Total preparation and cooking time: 40 minutes

This recipe does not freeze. The pastry ring can be made in advance, cooled, and stored in an airtight container until ready to serve. The pastry can be freshened in a hot oven for 5 minutes if required. The Pastry Cream can also be made in advance.

PASTRY TIP

After preparing the Pastry Cream, scrape the edge of the saucepan with a plate scraper, then press a piece of plastic wrap down onto the custard. This prevents a skin from forming.

Continental Fruit Ring

Palmiers

Palmiers

375g/12oz. puff pastry, thawed
½ cup/125g/4oz. sugar
1 cup/250ml/8fl. oz. cream, whipped
fresh berries

MAKES 24 SINGLE OR 12 FILLED

1. Roll out pastry to a 30cm x 25cm/12in. x 10in. oblong. Brush pastry sheet lightly with water and sprinkle with sugar.
2. Fold outside edges over to meet in centre; press down firmly. Fold the sides to the centre again. Make sure the two folded sides meet, then press firmly.
3. Cut into 1cm/½in. slices and space apart on a lightly greased baking sheet, cut-side down.
4. Bake in a very hot oven for 10 minutes or until golden brown. Cool.
5. If making filled palmiers, sandwich them together with whipped cream and berries.

Total preparation and cooking time: 20 minutes

This recipe suitable to freeze. Make up to the baking stage. Freeze flat on oven trays and bake when required.

Baklava

Memories of Athens

1½ cups/185g/6oz. ground almonds
½ cup/60g/2oz. finely chopped almonds
½ cup/125g/4oz. caster sugar
½ teaspoon freshly ground cardamom seeds
5 sheets filo pastry, thawed
60g/2oz. unsalted butter or margarine, melted
1 quantity warm syrup

MAKES APPROXIMATELY 18 PIECES

1. Combine first 4 ingredients; mix well.
2. Cut pastry sheets in half and trim to fit a 20cm/8in. square cake tin. Use 3 pieces of pastry, brush every second piece lightly with butter or margarine; line the base of the lightly greased tin.
3. Sprinkle ⅓ of the nut mixture over pastry. Top with 2 more pieces of buttered pastry. Continue in this way with remaining nuts and pastry, finishing with 3 buttered and layered sections of pastry.
4. With a sharp-bladed knife, slash the top into diamond-shaped pieces approximately 2.5cm/1in. wide. Sprinkle with cold water. Bake in a moderate oven for 25–30 minutes or until golden.
5. While still hot, pour warm syrup over baklava in tin. Allow to stand several hours before serving.
Syrup: Combine ¾ cup/185ml/6fl. oz. water, 1 cup/250g/8oz. sugar, 1 slice lemon and ¼ teaspoon ground cardamom in a saucepan. Bring to the boil, stirring until sugar dissolves. Simmer, uncovered for 15–20 minutes – do not stir. Remove from heat; allow to cool slightly. Remove lemon before using.

Total preparation and cooking time: 50 minutes

This recipe does not freeze.

PASTRY TIP

Filo is the Greek name for 'delicate, tissue-thin, opaque sheets of pastry'. Originally spelt 'phyllo', which derives from the Greek word *phyllon* meaning 'leaf'.

Baklava

Passionfruit Tart

Passionfruit Tart

185g/6oz. shortcrust pastry, thawed
¾ cup/185g/6oz. sugar
15g/½oz. butter or margarine
½ teaspoon finely grated lemon rind
2 eggs, separated
1 tablespoon lemon juice
2 tablespoons self-raising flour
½ cup/125ml/4fl. oz. passionfruit pulp
(about 6 fruit)
¾ cup/185ml/6fl. oz. milk
icing sugar

SERVES 6–8

1. Roll out pastry and use to line a lightly greased 23cm/9in. fluted flan tin; trim edges. Bake 'blind' in a moderately hot oven for 10 minutes, remove paper and baking beans and continue to cook pastry for a further 5 minutes.
2. Place sugar, margarine or butter, lemon rind and egg yolks in a bowl and beat for a few minutes until pale and thick. Stir in lemon juice then fold flour into mixture. Add passionfruit pulp and milk, mixing gently until ingredients are combined. Beat egg whites until stiff, and fold into mixture. Spoon filling into prepared pastry case.
3. Bake in a moderate oven for 40 minutes or until filling is golden and set. Cool tart, then dust with icing sugar.

Total preparation and cooking time: 75 minutes

This recipe does not freeze.

Fruit Tartlets

250g/8oz. shortcrust pastry, thawed
½ quantity Pastry Cream (see Continental
Fruit Ring, page 58) *or*
1 cup/250ml/8fl. oz. whipped cream
fresh or canned fruit
½ cup/125g/4oz. strawberry conserve, heated

MAKES 12

1. Roll out pastry and use to line 12 dome patty tins or small, fluted flan tins. Prick bases well and bake in a moderate oven for 15 minutes. Cool.
2. Place 1–2 teaspoonfuls of Pastry Cream or whipped cream in the base of each prepared tart shell. Decorate with fruit of your choice. Brush with strawberry jam.

Total preparation and cooking time: 40 minutes

This recipe does not freeze.

Fruit Tartlets

French Fruit Pastries

From my favourite patisserie

ready-rolled puff pastry sheets, thawed
prepared marzipan roll*
peach, pear or apricot halves; pitted cherries or
pineapple rings (cooked or canned)
beaten egg yolk
warm, sieved apricot jam

1. Roll out pastry sheets thinly. Place slices of marzipan on pastry and cover marzipan completely with selected fruits. Using a small, sharp knife cut around marzipan and fruit, leaving a 2cm/¾in. border of pastry.
2. Place pastries on a lightly greased baking sheet. Carefully brush only the pastry border with egg yolk.
3. Bake in a very hot oven for about 5 minutes or until pastry is crisp and golden.
4. Remove pastries to a wire rack and brush fruit only with apricot jam. Serve pastries warm or cold.
*A teaspoon of cream cheese can be used in place of a slice of marzipan.

Total preparation and cooking time: 15 minutes

This recipe does not freeze.

Mango & Banana Gallette

Tahitian surprise

2 sheets ready-rolled puff pastry, thawed
2 medium mangoes, peeled and sliced
1 medium banana, peeled and sliced
2 teaspoons sugar
beaten egg for glazing

SERVES 6

1. Roll out each pastry sheet thinly. Using a dinner plate as a guide, cut a circle of pastry out of each pastry sheet.
2. Place 1 circle of pastry on a lightly greased baking sheet. Arrange mango and banana on top of pastry; sprinkle lightly with half the sugar. Place pastry circle on top.
3. Mark top of pastry decoratively. Crimp edges. Glaze. Sprinkle with remaining sugar. Bake in a very hot oven for 10–15 minutes or until golden. Serve warm accompanied by whipped cream.

Total preparation and cooking time: 35 minutes

This recipe does not freeze.

French Fruit Pastries

FESTIVE DELIGHTS

For Christmas, Easter and other important party times, we have created this dazzling array of festive recipes that will delight your guests with their originality and wonderful range of flavours. And they're still time-saving enough to leave you leisure for enjoying the fun. Celebrate at your place and find out how easy it is!

Turkey Parcels

(with sage, rosemary and thyme)

6 turkey fillets
2 tablespoons chopped fresh parsley
½ teaspoon each dried sage, rosemary
and thyme *or*
2 teaspoons each of freshly chopped herbs
½ cup/60g/2oz. fresh white breadcrumbs
1 small rasher bacon, chopped
½ onion, finely chopped
2 tablespoons pine nuts
12 sheets filo pastry, thawed
2 teaspoons polyunsaturated oil

SERVES 6

1. Flatten turkey fillets, remove any sinews and cut a pocket in each fillet.
2. Combine herbs, breadcrumbs, bacon, onion and pine nuts.
3. Divide breadcrumb mixture between the 6 pockets in the turkey fillets.
4. Using 2 sheets of filo pastry, brush each sheet lightly with oil, layer, then fold in half. Repeat with remaining pastry.
5. Place a prepared turkey fillet on each portion of pastry. Roll turkey up in pastry, folding in the sides to form a parcel.
6. Place on an ungreased baking sheet; brush top lightly with oil.
7. Bake in a moderate oven for 15–20 minutes or until golden brown. Serve with cranberry sauce.

Cranberry Sauce

1 cup/250ml/8fl. oz. prepared cranberry sauce
¼ cup/60ml/2fl. oz. white wine

1. Combine all ingredients. Cook over gentle heat until warm.
To microwave:
Combine ingredients. Cook on high (100% power) for 1–2 minutes.

Total preparation and cooking time: 45 minutes

This recipe suitable to freeze. Prepare recipe up to the baking stage. Freeze and cook from frozen on day of serving, increasing cooking time by 15 minutes.

PASTRY TIP

Filo pastry is unique in that no added margarine or fat is used in the dough. The dough, which is very elastic in texture, is not rolled like other pastries but stretched to the desired thickness. This gives it its unique, delicate, tissue-thin, opaque sheets.

Easter Fish Slice

(or Russian Easter Pie)

30g/1oz. butter or margarine
½ cup/30g/1oz. chopped shallots or spring onions
2 cups/125g/4oz. roughly chopped mushrooms
¼ cup/30g/1oz. fresh breadcrumbs
freshly ground black pepper
2 x 375g/12oz. ocean trout or Atlantic salmon
fillets, skinned
500g/1lb puff pastry, thawed
2 hard-boiled eggs, chopped
½ cup/30g/1oz. chopped fresh parsley
beaten egg for glazing

SERVES 6

1. Melt butter or margarine; add shallots or spring onions, and mushrooms. Cook 2–3 minutes, remove from heat and stir in breadcrumbs. Season with pepper. Cool.
2. Remove any remaining bones in fish fillets, using tweezers.
3. Cut pastry into 2 pieces and roll out each piece to a 30cm x 20cm/12in. x 8in. oblong. Place 1 piece of pastry on a lightly greased baking sheet. Place 1 fillet of fish on pastry, top evenly with the cooled mushrooms, then a layer of egg and finally a layer of parsley. Place second fish fillet on top. Press together gently.
4. Brush edges of base pastry lightly with water. Top with remaining pastry, pressing together gently. Trim to a neat shape or cut into a fish shape. Decorate with extra pastry or mark with a sharp knife to give fish definition. Glaze.
5. Bake in a hot oven for 20 minutes or until golden brown. Serve hot or warm with a crisp salad or fresh vegetables.

Total preparation and cooking time: 50 minutes

This recipe does not freeze.

PASTRY TIP

Puff pastry, after baking, is a crisp, light pastry consisting of paper-thin layers of baked dough. These layers are prevented from sticking together by thin layers of margarine. While the pastry is baking, steam is caught between the layers of dough and forces them to rise. As the baking continues the steam evaporates and the margarine is absorbed, leaving a high, crisp, flaky pastry.

Easter Fish Slice

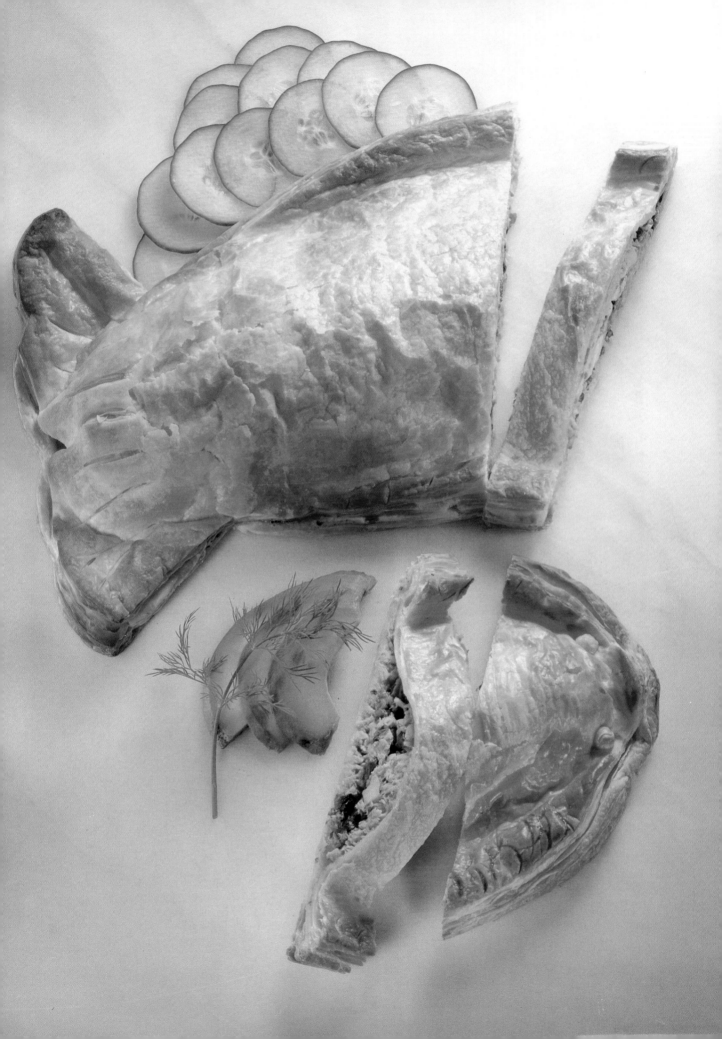

Baked Orange-Glazed Pork

Baked Orange-Glazed Pork

500g/1lb piece smoked loin of pork
1½ tablespoons grainy mustard
1 tablespoon orange marmalade
finely grated rind of 1 orange
185g/6oz. puff pastry, thawed
beaten egg for glazing

SERVES 6–8

1. Cut pork in half lengthwise. Score the top
by cutting diagonal slits one way and then the other.
2. Combine mustard, marmalade and orange
rind. Brush the mustard mixture evenly along
the scored area of pork.
3. Roll out pastry thinly to a large oblong.

4. Place pork in centre of pastry. Brush all pastry
edges lightly with water. Fold pastry over pork.
Fold edges up to enclose pork.
5. Glaze with beaten egg. Bake in a hot oven
for 30 minutes or until golden brown. Serve
with vegetables or salad.

Total preparation and cooking time: 60 minutes

This recipe does not freeze.

PASTRY TIP
Use leftover pastry as garnishes or decorations
on pies or as croutons in soups and casseroles
or as snacks.

Boxing Day Twist

A leftovers triumph

10 sheets filo pastry, thawed
2 teaspoons polyunsaturated oil
beaten egg for glazing
sesame seeds

TURKEY TWIST
2 cups/250g/8oz. minced or finely chopped
cooked turkey
½ cup/60g/2oz. fresh white breadcrumbs
¼ cup/60ml/2fl. oz. cranberry sauce
1 tablespoon mayonnaise
1 tablespoon chopped fresh parsley
1 egg
ground black pepper

HAM TWIST
2½ cups /315g/10oz. minced or finely chopped ham
½ cup/60g/2oz. fresh white breadcrumbs
¼ cup/60ml/2fl. oz. mayonnaise
1 tablespoon chopped fresh parsley
1 egg
ground black pepper

SERVES 6–8

1. In separate bowls combine all the Turkey Twist ingredients and the Ham Twist ingredients. Mix well.
2. Brush every second sheet of pastry lightly with oil and layer 5 sheets together. Repeat with remaining 5 sheets, finishing with two separate stacks of pastry.
3. Spoon turkey filling down one stack of pastry, leaving 3cm/1¼in. at ends. Roll up firmly, folding in the edges. Repeat with remaining pastry and the ham filling.
4. Twist the two rolls together and place on a lightly greased baking sheet. Brush with egg glaze and sprinkle with sesame seeds.
5. Bake in a moderately hot oven for 25–30 minutes or until golden. Serve hot.

Total preparation and cooking time: 60 minutes

This recipe suitable to freeze. Prepare recipe up to the baking stage. Freeze. Bake from frozen on day of serving, increasing cooking time by 10 minutes.

Festive Pork Roll

500g/1lb lean pork mince
1 clove garlic, crushed
2 teaspoons finely chopped fresh ginger
2 teaspoons soy sauce
2 teaspoons sherry
2 tablespoons chopped fresh coriander
ground black pepper
4 shallots or spring onions, chopped
¼ medium red capsicum (pepper), cut into strips
1 small stick celery, cut into strips
⅓ cup/75g/2½oz. water chestnuts, sliced
8 sheets filo pastry, thawed
2 teaspoons polyunsaturated oil

SERVES 6

1. Combine pork mince, garlic, ginger, soy sauce, sherry, coriander and pepper. Mix well.
2. Place meat mixture on a sheet of plastic wrap, 32cm x 18cm/12¾in. x 7in. and press out meat to the edges of plastic. Place shallots or spring onions, capsicum, celery and water chestnuts on top of meat. Roll up, Swiss Roll style, peeling off plastic wrap at each turn.
3. Brush every second sheet of pastry lightly with oil, and layer. Place the pork roll on the end of the pastry stack. Roll up, folding in ends.
4. Place on a lightly greased baking sheet. Brush top lightly with oil.
5. Bake in a moderately hot oven for 25–30 minutes or until golden brown. Serve hot with spicy sauce.

Total preparation and cooking time: 60 minutes

This recipe does not freeze.

Spicy Sauce

¼ cup/60g/2oz. sugar
¾ cup/185ml/6fl. oz. water
2 teaspoons minced chilli, or to taste
2 tablespoons tomato paste (purée)
2 teaspoons soy sauce
1 tablespoon white vinegar
1 teaspoon finely chopped fresh ginger
1 tablespoon cornflour

MAKES 1 CUP/250ML/8FL. OZ.

1. Blend cornflour and ½ cup/125ml/4fl. oz. water in a small saucepan. Add remaining ingredients and bring to the boil, stirring continuously. Serve hot.
To microwave:
Blend cornflour and ½ cup/125ml/4fl. oz. water to a paste in a microwave-safe bowl. Add remaining ingredients and cook on high (100% power) for approximately 2 minutes. Stir after each 30 seconds or until sauce is thick.

Cherry & Almond Gâteau

Cherry & Almond Gâteau

Elegant and easy

½ cup/125ml/4fl. oz. boiling water
75g/2½oz. packet quick custard mix
½ cup/60g/2oz. ground almonds, toasted
2 sheets ready-rolled puff pastry, thawed
410g/13oz. can stoned black cherries, well drained
beaten egg for glazing

SERVES 4–6

1. Using only ½ cup/125ml/4fl. oz. boiling water, make up contents of pack of quick custard mix according to directions on pack. Allow to cool completely.
2. Fold toasted ground almonds through cold, thick custard.
3. Roll out each sheet of pastry thinly and with a sharp knife, cut two 25cm/10in. discs. Place one disc on baking sheet.
4. Spread cold almond filling over pastry disc to within 4cm/1¾in. of edges. Arrange well-drained cherries on almond filling.
5. Place second disc on top, gently pressing down edges. Glaze.
6. With the point of a knife, mark the top with faint arc-shape lines radiating from the centre. Score or scallop pastry edges.
7. Bake in a very hot oven for 20–30 minutes or until pastry is golden brown. If desired, immediately gâteau is removed from oven, sprinkle liberally with icing sugar. Serve with cream or ice-cream.

Total preparation and cooking time: 45 minutes

This recipe does not freeze.

PASTRY TIP

Do not allow the prepared, unbaked pastry dish to stand too long or in too warm a place prior to baking.

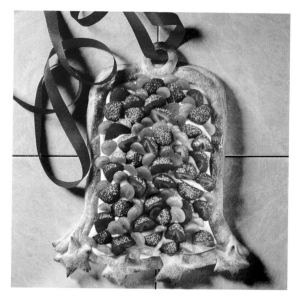

Christmas Fruit Bell

Christmas Fruit Bell

3 sheets ready-rolled puff pastry, thawed
egg white, lightly beaten
granulated sugar
300ml/10fl. oz. double cream
1 teaspoon vanilla essence
fresh or canned fruits
icing sugar

SERVES 4–6

1. Roll out each sheet of pastry thinly. Cut 3 identical, large bell shapes from the sheets of pastry.
2. Place one bell on baking sheet and prick thoroughly. Brush bell lightly with water. With remaining two shapes, cut out centre, leaving a 2cm/¾in. border. While maintaining bell shape, remove inner shape and set aside for use as decoration.
3. Place bell-shaped pastry frames carefully on pastry bell on baking sheet.
4. Cut small, fancy shapes from set-aside pastry and decorate the base of the bell. Cut a circle for the bell handle and arrange on pastry bell.

Traditional Fruit Mince Tarts

5. Brush lightly with beaten egg white, then sprinkle liberally with sugar.
6. Bake in a hot oven for 25–30 minutes, until pastry is golden.
7. Remove to a wire rack to cool completely.
8. Lightly whip cream with vanilla essence; spoon into pastry bell. Decorate with fresh or canned fruits. Dust with icing sugar.

Total preparation and cooking time: 60 minutes

This recipe does not freeze. The pastry bell can be made in advance, stored in an airtight container and filled when ready to serve. The pastry can be freshened in a hot oven for 5 minutes if required.

Traditional Fruit Mince Tarts

250g/8oz. shortcrust pastry, thawed
2 cups/500g/1lb prepared fruit mince
1–2 tablespoons granulated sugar (optional)

MAKES 20

1. Roll out pastry thinly. Using a 7.5cm/3in. fluted or plain cutter, cut 20 discs from shortcrust pastry sheet and 20 rounds using a 6cm/2½in. cutter. Line patty tins with larger rounds.
2. Divide fruit mince equally between pastry cases, pressing down gently with the back of a spoon. Place a pastry disc on each filled pastry case.
3. Lightly brush tops with water; sprinkle with sugar if desired.
4. Bake in a moderately hot oven for 15–20 minutes or until golden. Dust tops with icing sugar if desired. Serve warm or cold.

Variations

Place slices of almond paste (marzipan) on top of fruit mince instead of pastry. Or, bake as directed, then drizzle cold cooked pies with melted chocolate.

Total preparation and cooking time: 35 minutes

This recipe suitable to freeze.

Rocky Road Tartlets

100g/3½oz. dark chocolate
15g/½oz. butter or margarine
1 cup/125g/4oz. quartered marshmallows
¼ cup/60g/2oz. halved red and green glacé cherries
¼ cup/30g/1oz. roughly chopped pecans
12 ready-made sweet shortcrust tartlet cases, *or*
19cm/7½in. ready-made sweet shortcrust pastry case
icing sugar

MAKES 12

1. Melt chocolate and butter or margarine in a bowl set over a pan of simmering water. Remove from heat and stir in marshmallows, cherries and pecans.
To microwave:
Place chocolate and butter or margarine in a microwave-safe bowl. Cook on high (100% power) for 1–2 minutes. Stir at 30-second intervals until chocolate has melted. Remove from oven.
2. Divide rocky road mixture between the tartlet cases or large pastry case; allow to set in refrigerator.
3. Sprinkle with icing sugar to serve.

Total preparation and cooking time: 40 minutes

This recipe does not freeze.

Christmas Crumble Puffs

90g/3oz. butter or margarine
¾ cup/90g/3oz. plain flour
¾ cup/185g/6oz. fruit mince
1 teaspoon ground cinnamon
4 sheets ready-rolled puff pastry, thawed
icing sugar

MAKES APPROXIMATELY 30

1. Rub butter or margarine into flour. Stir in fruit mince and cinnamon. Mix well.
2. Roll out each pastry sheet to a 23cm/9in. square. Lightly brush one pastry sheet with water. Prick with fork. Top with second pastry sheet. Repeat with remaining pastry.
3. Cut 15 medium-sized shapes from both sandwiched puff-pastry sheets. Spoon approximately 1 teaspoonful of fruit mince mixture onto each pastry shape.
4. Place on a lightly greased baking tray. Bake in a hot oven for 12–18 minutes or until pastry is golden.
5. Serve warm or cold, sprinkled with icing sugar.

Total preparation and cooking time: 35 minutes

This recipe does not freeze.

Rocky Road Tartlets   Christmas Crumble Puffs
Boxing Day Twist   Recipe, page 67

PASTRY TECHNIQUES

Your step-by-step guide to making the most of the delicious
possibilities from pastries. Practical, tempting
and decorative ideas, plus recommended oven temperatures
and baking techniques for perfect results.

BLIND BAKING OR PRE-BAKING PASTRY CASES FOR CRISPNESS

Blind baking literally means to bake without a filling. There are two types of blind baking – partial baking and full baking.

Partial baking is for pastry cases which are filled and baked again; this preliminary baking sets the pastry and is a safeguard against soggy-based pastry crusts when an especially moist filling is to be baked in the pastry case, such as quiche fillings, custard or fruits.

Fully baked pastry cases are used for savoury or sweet pre-cooked cold fillings, such as lemon meringue, or fillings such as fruits, gelatine-set fillings or savoury fillings.

TO BLIND BAKE

It is important to remember that blind baking and, in particular, the use of the 'loading' plays the important role in achieving good-looking partially baked or fully baked pastry cases. It is the 'loading' that supports or keeps the sides of the pastry in place while baking. Because the pastry is collapsible (when subjected to the oven heat) until the pastry has set (or is firm) the pastry must be held in place against the sides of the pie or flan dish. This is achieved by the 'loading' (dried peas, beans or rice all make convenient weights – kept specially for this purpose, as they can be re-used again and again).

Baking Guidelines
Pastry should be baked in a pre-heated oven.

Partially Bake (quiches, custard tarts, meat or fruit pies)
1. Lightly grease dull, dark flan tin, ring or pie plate. (Use dull, dark metal dishes.)

2. Lay the rolled-out pastry sheet(s) in dish. Press the pastry lightly into the base of the dish with the fingers, lift the edges of the pastry slightly away from the sides of the dish with the fingers, then gently push the pastry against the side, working from the base upwards, being careful not to pull, stretch or decrease the pastry thickness.
3. Trim off the excess pastry and crimp edges.
4. Line the pastry case with two thicknesses of lightly greased greaseproof, brown paper or foil well up the sides. Cover the base with dried beans, peas, rice, pasta or metal pastry weights (loading), then gently push them up the sides to keep the pastry quite firmly in place during the baking. (This prevents the pastry sides from collapsing.)
5. Bake in a pre-heated oven: see Baking Guidelines.
6. Remove paper or foil and loading. Refer to the appropriate recipe, add filling and complete baking.
7. Remove from oven and place on a wire rack to cool.

Fully Bake (fresh fruit tarts, lemon meringue, gelatine-set, cold sweet and savoury tarts)
1. Follow directions outlined in 'Partially Bake' numbers 1. to 3. then:
4. Prick the base of the pastry with a fork.
5. Line the pastry case with two thicknesses of lightly greased greaseproof, brown paper or foil, extending the paper or foil well up the sides. Cover the base with dried beans, peas, rice, pasta or metal pastry weights (loading), then gently push them up the sides to keep the pastry quite firmly in place during the baking. (This prevents the pastry sides from collapsing).
6. Bake in a pre-heated oven: see Baking Guidelines.

NOTE: Pastry cannot be blind baked in a microwave oven successfully.

SHORTCRUST AND WHOLEMEAL
Partially baked:
- conventional oven, moderately hot (190°C/375°F) for 15 minutes,
- fan-assisted oven, moderate (180°C/350°F) for 10 minutes.

Fully baked:
- conventional oven, moderately hot (190°C/375°F) for 15 minutes, remove paper or foil and loading, continue baking for a further 5–10 minutes, until pastry is pale golden in colour,
- fan-assisted oven, moderate (180°C/350°F) for 10 minutes, remove paper or foil and loading, continue baking for a further 5–8 minutes, until pastry is pale golden in colour.

SWEET SHORTCRUST
Partially baked:
- conventional oven, moderate (180°C/350°F) for 15 minutes,
- fan-assisted oven, moderately slow (160°C/325°F) for 10 minutes.

Fully baked:
- conventional oven, moderate (180°C/350°F) for 15 minutes, remove paper or foil and loading, continue baking for a further 5–10 minutes, until pastry is pale golden in colour,
- fan-assisted oven, moderately slow (160°C/325°F) for 10 minutes, remove paper or foil and loading, continue baking for 5–10 minutes, until pastry is pale golden in colour.

FILO
Partially baked:
- because of the characteristics of filo pastry, it is not necessary to blind bake filo pastry prior to adding a filling.

Fully baked:
- it is not necessary to blind bake filo pastry as suggested for short-crust, wholemeal or sweet short-crust. Simply lay thawed, buttered and layered sheets (at least 4–5 sheets) in dish. Press lightly into the base and against sides, being careful not to tear pastry, then neaten edges by folding under or over, then press lightly onto rim of dish.
- conventional oven, moderate (180°C/350°F) for 15–18 minutes, until pastry is a rich, light golden brown colour.
- fan-assisted oven, moderately slow (160°C/325°F) for 12–15 minutes, until pastry is a rich, light golden brown colour.

PASTRY GLAZING

Glazing is a technique used to enhance the overall appearance and taste of pastry dishes, and can be employed in two ways.

1. Glazing prior to baking – which produces colour, gloss and texture during baking.
2. Glazing after baking – which produces brilliance, glitter and flavour and acts as a simple icing.

GLAZING PRIOR TO BAKING

Egg wash (beaten egg): Produces a high gloss and golden colour when baked. Lightly beat one egg with one tablespoon cold water and ¼–½ teaspoon salt.

Cream, milk or water: An economical glaze which you simply brush on to improve the finished appearance of the baked products.

Custard powder: An economical glaze which adds additional colour. Mix one teaspoon custard powder to a smooth paste with a little of the milk (¼ cup/60ml/2fl. oz.) then add remaining milk.

Coffee: Adds rich, golden colour. Dissolve ¼ cup/60g/2oz. granulated sugar in ¼ cup/60ml/2fl. oz. hot, strong coffee.

Melted butter and sugar (or salt): Produces a light brown crust. Brush with melted butter or margarine and sprinkle with 2–4 teaspoons granulated sugar (for sweet), 1–2 teaspoons rock salt (for savoury).

GLAZING AFTER BAKING

Glacé icing: Made up of water, vanilla essence and icing sugar, this mixture produces a semi-transparent glaze. It is brushed on immediately the baked product is removed from the oven (unless otherwise directed in the recipe).

Conserve or jam glaze: Gives a delightful sparkle to pastry tops. Hot boiled conserve or jam, strained, is brushed onto the pastry immediately the baked product is removed from the oven.

PASTRY DECORATION

Puff pastry pie edge (scalloping)

Place band of pastry around rim of pie dish.

Assemble pie funnel and pastry lid and trim. Decorate by 'scalloping' pie edge. Place thumb and forefinger on rim, and using dull edge of knife indent pastry between fingers.

Then pull knife upwards through the 2 layers of pastry. Repeat at intervals around rim, forming a scalloped edge.

Pastry trellis

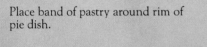

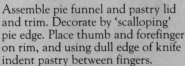

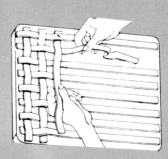

Cut strips of pastry with pastry wheel or sharp knife.

Using the pastry sleeve as backing, form trellis by weaving pastry strips. This avoids doing it straight on the pie, which can be very messy.

Position on rim of assembled pie and carefully remove by holding edge and gradually drawing off pack, then trim.

FILO HANDY HINTS

Step 1
Totally thaw filo pastry as recommended on the pack. For best results thaw overnight in a refrigerator and then for one hour at room temperature prior to use. Unfold. Carefully separate the required number of sheets as a stack as specified in the individual recipe. Re-wrap unused pastry in a freezer bag.

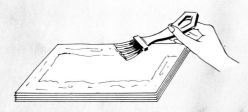

Step 2
Quickly, but lightly, brush edges of first sheet of filo pastry with melted butter, margarine or oil.

Step 3
Then brush centre area of filo pastry sheet lightly with melted butter or margarine.

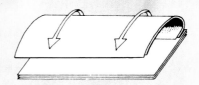

Step 4
Carefully pick up the top sheet you have just buttered, turn it over and place it back on the remaining stack. It will now stick to the next sheet. Butter the side now face up (as in steps 2 and 3).

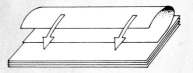

Step 5
Now pick up the top two sheets and again turn over and place back on the stack. Butter the side now face up (as in steps 2 and 3). Now pick up the top three sheets, turn over and butter. Continue working down through the stack in this way, progressively picking up more and more sheets as you butter and layer, until you have reached the bottom and buttered all the sheets.

Why butter and layer filo pastry?
Filo pastry is unique. In order to make filo pastry light and flaky when baked, it is essential that each (or alternate) sheet be brushed with melted butter, margarine or oil before baking so that, in baking, the sheets separate to create a light and flaky pastry.
The above steps illustrate how to prepare filo, buttering every sheet. If you desire less butter in your recipes, we recommend buttering every second sheet (treating two sheets as one when referring to the steps above). This method is specifically designed to allow you to butter sheets quickly and therefore minimise sheets drying out during preparation.

VOL-AU-VENTS

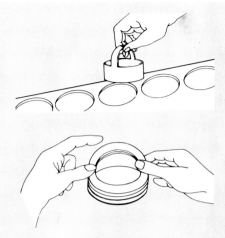

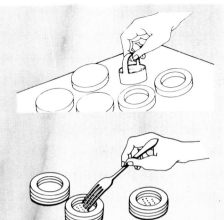

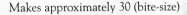

Makes approximately 30 (bite-size)

Vol-au-vents (patty shells) are airy cups of puff pastry that can range in size; tiny for a bite-size at the cocktail hour, or medium-sized for entrée or for holding fresh and tantalising dessert-type fillings, or as large as a dinner plate to hold savoury or sweet fillings to serve 6–8.
An important instrument in creating the vol-au-vent is a good, sharp-edged cutter or knife that will cut cleanly without dragging or twisting the pastry.

Ingredients
500g/1lb packet puff pastry, thawed egg wash*, milk or cream

Method
1. Pre-heat
   - conventional oven to very hot (230°C/450°F),
   - fan-assisted oven to hot (200°C/400°F).
2. Cut thawed puff pastry into three equal pieces and roll out to a 2.5mm/1/8in. thickness
3. Using a 5cm/2in. round, oval or square, plain or fluted sharp cutter or knife, using even pressure, cut 30 discs from one piece of pastry. Turn discs upside-down on an ungreased baking sheet; lightly brush with water.
4. With another piece, lightly brush with water, then top with remaining pastry piece.
5. Cut into 30 discs, matching the base pastry.
6. Then, with a smaller cutter, cut an inner circle, remove and set aside**.
7. Place pastry ring carefully on base; with a fork, prick base of pastry.
8. Brush top surface of ring lightly with egg wash, milk or cream.

9. Bake in pre-heated
   - conventional oven for about 10–15 minutes.
   - fan-assisted oven for about 7–12 minutes, until pastry top is golden brown in colour and sides are brown and crisp.

RE-HEATING INSTRUCTIONS
The sooner the vol-au-vent cases can be filled and served, the fresher, lighter and more delicious they will be. However, they can be re-heated if serving the same day, or frozen. Wrap in freezer bags or freezer wrap. Make airtight, seal, label and freeze.

To re-heat unfilled: Pre-heat
- conventional oven to hot (200°C/400°F),
- fan-assisted oven to moderately hot (190°C/375°F).
Place unfilled vol-au-vents in oven for 3–5 minutes, turn off heat and, within 8–10 minutes, vol-au-vents will be crisp.

To re-heat filled: Pre-heat
- conventional oven to moderate (180°C/350°F),
- fan-assisted oven to moderately slow (160°C/325°F).
Place filled vol-au-vents in oven for about 15–20 minutes.

*Egg wash: lightly beat one egg with one tablespoon cold water and 1/4–1/2 teaspoon salt (produces a professional baker's glaze).
**Inner pastry discs can be baked and used for decoration on completed vol-au-vents, or lightly brushed with water and tossed in bruised sesame, poppy or caraway seeds (bruising seeds helps to release their full flavour on baking) and used for party nibbles, as is, or with your favourite dip.

TO MAKE PUFF PASTRY TOPS FOR INDIVIDUAL SERVES OF SOUP, CASSEROLES OR FRUIT DESSERTS

1. Using the serving dishes as a guide, cut pastry to fit over the serving dishes, allowing a 2.5cm/1in. border.

2. Place pastry on top of serving dish; pinch edges.
3. Bake in a hot oven for 20–25 minutes, or until pastry is puffed and golden.

TO PREPARE FILO TRIANGLES WITH SWEET AND SAVOURY FILLINGS

1. Cut filo pastry sheets into strips (six strips for small cocktail savouries or three strips for more hearty serves). Using three strips for each puff, brush every second sheet lightly with oil.
2. Place one tablespoon of mixture on the bottom right-hand corner of each strip; fold the corner over to form a triangle. Continue folding to the end of the strip – retaining shape with each fold.

3. Place puffs, with the last fold underneath, on a lightly greased tray. Brush pastry tops lightly with oil. Bake in a moderately hot oven for 15–20 minutes or until golden.

TO MAKE GATHERED FILO PARCELS

1. Cut filo pastry sheets in half. Using four half-sheets for each parcel, brush every second sheet lightly with oil.
2. Place filling (sweet or savoury) in centre of pastry. Taking the four sheets of pastry, draw the four corners up, and gently press together to form a pouch.

3. Brush the outside of the parcel lightly with oil; place on a lightly greased baking sheet. Bake in a moderately hot oven.

TO PREPARE A ROUND OR SQUARE PASTRY DISH WITHOUT USING A PIE TIN

1. Roll out puff or shortcrust pastry. Then cut out 2 x 24cm/9½in. circles (use a plate as a guide). Place one round on a lightly greased baking sheet.

2. Spread filling – sweet or savoury – leaving a 2.5cm/1in. border. Moisten border with water and place second sheet of pastry on top. Crimp edges.
3. Glaze and bake.

TO PREPARE AND ROLL
A FILO STRUDEL

1. Using approximately 10 sheets of filo pastry, brush every second sheet lightly with butter, margarine or oil, and layer.
2. Spoon filling (sweet or savoury) down the centre of the pastry, leaving a 10cm/4in. border at each end of pastry.

3. Fold pastry edges into the centre, over filling, tuck ends in and fold the pastry over filling to make a roll.
4. Place roll seam-side down on an ungreased baking tray. Brush top lightly with butter, margarine or oil. With a sharp knife cut deep diagonal slits across pastry top.
5. Bake in a moderately hot oven.

TO PREPARE A PLAITED LOAF

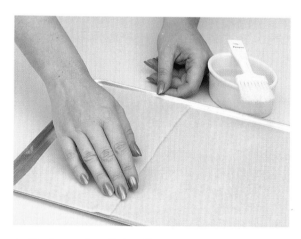

1. If using ready-rolled puff pastry sheets roll out each sheet to an equal size. Brush one edge of pastry sheet with water and overlap with the other sheet of pastry. Press edges together lightly.
2. Spoon filling (sweet or savoury) down centre of pastry, forming mixture into a log shape.

3. Brush edges of pastry lightly with water. Cut pastry on either side of filling into diagonal 1cm/½in. strips. Lift alternate strips over filling to resemble a plait. Glaze and bake.

OVEN TEMPERATURES

	Gas	Electricity
Slow	150°C (300°F)	150°C (300°F)
Moderately Slow	160°C (325°F)	170°C (330°F)
Moderate	180°C (350°F)	200°C (400°F)
Moderately Hot	190°C (375°F)	220°C (425°F)
Hot	200°C (400°F)	230°C (450°F)
Very Hot	230°C (450°F)	250°C (475°F)

Recipes feature measurements based on a standard 250ml cup and 20ml tablespoon.

RECOMMENDED BAKING TEMPERATURES AND TIMES

These are general guidelines; look at individual recipes for temperatures and times specific to the recipe.

Puff Pastry – Pre-heated, very hot (230°C/450°F) oven. Baking times will vary according to use (all recipes included in the book give suggested baking times).

Shortcrust – Pre-heated, moderately hot (190°C/375°F) oven. Baking times will vary according to use. If soft, moist fillings, such as egg custard (quiche, custard tarts) or fruit fillings, are placed in an unbaked pastry case the first 10 minutes of baking time should be in a pre-heated, very hot (230°C/450°F) oven, unless otherwise stated in the recipe. This allows the pastry to lightly set and not soak up moisture from the filling and become soggy.

Sweet Shortcrust – Pre-heated, moderate (180°C/350°F) oven. Baking times will vary according to use. Wholemeal – Pre-heated, moderately hot (190°C/375°F) oven. Baking times will vary according to use. Filo – Pre-heated, moderate (180°C/350°F) oven. Baking times will vary according to use. Filo pastry is baked when the top is golden brown in colour and the layers have risen, as with puff pastry but not as high.

INDEX